REINHARD HEYDRICH

THE BIOGRAPHY

VOLUME I
ROAD TO WAR

MAX WILLIAMS

ULRIC of ENGLAND

ISBN 0 9537577 5 7

ULRIC PUBLISHING
P.O.BOX 55
CHURCH STRETTON
SHROPSHIRE
SY6 6WR
ENGLAND

TELEPHONE: 01694 781354
FACSIMILE: 01694 781372

E- mail: books @ ulric-publishing.com

www.ulric-publishing.com

GRAPHICS & LAYOUT BY ULRIC DESIGN

First published in 2001 by ULRIC PUBLISHING

INDEX

FOREWORD

The objective of this book is to define fact from fiction, in the short and extraordinary life of Reinhard Heydrich. To achieve this aim, the authors sourced and evaluated previously unpublished information, (including documents and photographs from numerous private archives), relating to both Heydrich's political and personal life. As a result, the reader is presented, for the first time, with both an objective and comprehensive picture.

Information was collated over some ten years. In some instances however, the authors were too late, and the march of progress had destroyed irreplaceable, historical treasures. The site of Heydrich's birth place in Halle for example is now a shopping complex. Additionally, a reply from the Bulovka Hospital, Prague, confirmed all medical records of 1942 had been destroyed in a flood caused by the development of a new metro station.

Several existing sources failed to honour requests for factual information; a letter of enquiry to the Luftwaffe Museum in Uetersen, Germany, regarding Heydrich's meritous war service with the Luftwaffe (he was awarded both classes of Iron Cross, the coveted Pilots' Badge, plus the Bronze and Silver bars for combat missions[1]) received short shrift; Heydrich was described as *"....not the sort of man the Luftwaffe would wish to be associated with"* [2].

A request for a copy of Heydrichs' marriage certificate from the Registrar at Grossenbrode also met a blank refusal (a law exists in Germany, which forbids the use of private certificates without permission of the surviving relatives). Inspite of not experiencing any difficulties with the authorities in Halle and a valiant effort by the British Embassy in Bonn, the outcome remained unchanged [3].

Mention must also be made here of the surviving members of the Heydrich family, who were initially contacted via a third party, and later by the authors. Both occasions were met with a negative response, and following the death of Heydrich's wife, Lina, in 1985, it would understandably seem the family wish to maintain a lower profile. This then is the reason for the lack of early photographs from the Halle era.

To date, only two of the post war biographies attempt to paint a true, historical picture. Günther Deschner's 'Heydrich – The Pursuit of Total Power' and Lina Heydrich's ' Leben mit einem Kriegsverbrecher' (Living With A War Criminal). Deschner's book offers much information gained from personal interviews with Heydrich's widow and various Heydrich associates, while Lina Heydrich's book offers personal detail about her late husband and her view of the National Socialist leadership. Both of these excellent works have been utilised as source material for this study.

The early attempt by the British writer Charles Wighton, 'Heydrich – Hitler's Most Evil Henchman' is ill informed, and in places, factually incorrect. It is however, an acceptable study considering Wighton did not have access to much of the information available to day. Two further biographies, are governed by popular misrepresentations and lack objectivity; the 1982 edition of 'Reinhard Heydrich' by the German journalist Edouard Calic, and the more recent publication 'Heydrich - Henchman of Death' by Charles Whiting.

It is hoped that this study will dispel the myths associated with Reinhard Heydrich's life, and in turn, offer an informative biography to both the specialised historian and general reader.

MAX WILLIAMS
ULRIC of ENGLAND

ACKNOWLEDGEMENTS

We extend our sincere thanks to all those who, in our effort to produce an objective work, contributed to the manuscript, (including names who wish to remain anonymous), and in particular;

Special mention must be made of the following individuals:

Norman "Harry" Harrison who accompanied one of the authors on numerous archive and related visits both at home and abroad, sharing both highs and lows of discoveries. Without his company, many of the visits to foreign parts would not conjure up such fond memories.

Kerstin Seemann spent many hours translating sometimes difficult passages from her mother tongue into English. To her we extend our special thanks.

Rod Tidnam, our photographer for his technical excellence - without his expertise this volume would be a far less attractive proposition. Our gratitude is immeasurable.

H.R. in Prague, for guiding us through a large quantity of material, The two volumes would not contain so many excellent photographs without her help.

Dr. Miroslav Ivanov, also of Prague, assisted us with responses to questions only somebody with his authoritative knowledge could have answered.

Ian Sayer allowed unrestricted access to his vast archive of original documents relating to the Second World War.

K.....for opening the door of his unique photographic archive.

Mention must also be made of the help extended by the following:

Peter Ashworth
Bruno Binding
David Chandler
Jaroslav Cvancara
Rudy A. D'Angelo
Dr. Richard A. Davis
Larry Deveraux
Dr. Andreas Eckert
Peter Etherington
Malcolm Fisher
Roger Forrow
Pastor O. Göldner
Heider Hammer
Hugo Haig-Thomas
Olga Harris
Hans H. Hildebrand
Dr. James B. Kahn
Lesley Kress
Nikolas von Lindenau †
Robin Lumsden
Callum MacDonald
Joanna Morel
Bob Moses
Sylvia Rogge
Stuart Russell
Heinrich W. Schild
Andrea Schumann
Angela Schüttrup
Verne E. Schwartz

Keith Slade
Andreas Thies
James Townsend †
Alec Walker
Dr. B.C. West †
Larry Whitehill
Ray Zyla

and the staff of the following institutions:

Document Centre, US Mission, Berlin
Bundesarchiv, Koblenz
Standesamt, Halle
Stadtarchiv, Halle
State Archives, Prague
State Army Archives, Prague
National Archives, Washington DC
Library of Congress, Washington DC
Yivo Institute, New York
Public Records Office, Kew
German Naval Academy, Flensburg
Marine-Offizier-Vereinigung, Bonn
The Wiener Library, London
Bayerisches Hauptstaatsarchiv, Munich
Staatsbibliothek, Munich

INTRODUCTION

Who was Reinhard Heydrich, and why, some sixty years after his assasination in 1942, does he continue to generate so much interest ?

During his relatively short life, Heydrich became a controversial, enigmatic character, and ingenious diplomatic negotiator. His subordinates were often amazed at the extent of his memory and his ability to quickly understand difficult reports which had taken hours to prepare. Heydrich's breadth of talent excelled beyond his Party and government posts, to the sports field and musical arts.

His life had been one of controversy, which still continues to this day. Labelled by some as the author of the 'final solution' to the Jewish question, Heydrich has been branded as a 20th century Machiavellian. Others in admiration of his intelligence, sporting and musical talents, have bestowed upon him the iconic status of a Renaissance man.

Assasinated at the pinnacle of his success, SS-Obergruppenführer Heydrich was afforded a state funeral in the Mosaic Room of the new Reich Chancellery. the Führer and Reichchancellor of the Third German Reich, Adolf Hitler, patted the cheeks of the dead mans' children, and absent-mindedly muttered *"Heydrich, he was a man with a heart of iron"* [1]. Eleven years before his death, at the age of 27, Heydrich was an unemployed, ex-naval officer with little or no prospects. How could he have attained the position as possible heir apparent to the most powerful man in Europe - Adolf Hitler.

CHAPTER 1
THE FORMATIVE YEARS

Reinhard Tristan Eugen Heydrich was born on 7th March 1904 at Marienstrasse 21, in the Saxony town of Halle on the Saale River. He was christened in the Catholic faith four days later at St. Elizabeth's Church in Mauerstrasse. The names were chosen by both parents: Reinhard, by his mother Elisabeth (after a character in one of her husband's operas), Tristan, by his father Bruno, (after the opera by Wagner) and Eugen after his maternal grandfather.

Bruno Heydrich was born in 1863 in the town of Leuben, the eldest son of a family of seven, the other children all being girls. He had an interest in music from an early age and began serious study at the age of twelve in Meissen. His main instruments included the violin, tenor horn, tuba and double bass, and by the age of thirteen he was already making public appearances. As a soloist in the Meissen Youth Orchestra, in 1882, Bruno completed a three year scholarship, with honours, in the double bass at the Royal Conservatoire in Dresden. He followed this with work in the orchestra of Hans von Bülow, and from 1883 until 1887, was the double bass soloist with the Royal Orchestra in Dresden. His goal was to become bandmaster and conductor, he studied under Professor Doctor Wüllner who encouraged his talent as a singer. A recommendation to the Weimar Court Theatre as court opera singer followed, providing him with opportunities for successful appearances as Lohengrin, Walter von Stolzing and Tristan at several of the leading opera houses in Germany. Cosima Wagner familiarised Bruno Heydrich with Wagner's style for a few weeks in the summer of 1890, it is believed that she gave him with a jewel encrusted gold swan, which he wore on his tie for many years. Unfortunately Bruno's aspiration to appear at Wagner's Bayreuth never materialised, as he failed to attain the highest echelons of the singing world, always remaining just that little short of ultimate success.

Bruno Heydrich

His failed ambition to succeed as a maestro singer encouraged him to focus on composing and it is this talent which presented him success. In 1895, his operatic work 'Amen' received critical acclaim, followed by 'Peace' in 1907 and 'Chance' in 1914. He continued with various orchestral, choral and chamber works which, although never reaching the pinnacle of success, guarantied his recognition in musical circles.

During his studies at the Dresden Conservatoire of Music Bruno Heydrich met and fell in love with the director's daughter, Elisabeth Marie Anna Amalia Krantz. She was small, blonde, blue-eyed, groomed and cultured and had excellent prospects. He was tall, of heavy stature with black locks of hair, jocular and rather loud, the exact opposite of the restrained young lady towards whom he directed his attentions. In December 1897, they were married and Bruno, aged thirty-four, at last achieved acceptance into the high ranks of society.

Elisabeth's father, Eugen Krantz, was professor of music, a Royal Saxony Councillor and founder of the Dresden Conservatoire of Music, which attained world renown. Of his three children, only Elisabeth had aspirations in the world of music, the two boys looking elsewhere for their interests. She had set her sights on the lucrative conservatoire and when one of her father's pupils displayed a keen interest in her, her future looked comfortable.

Born in Dresden in 1871, Elisabeth received a convent education and remained a strict Catholic throughout her life. She was schooled in music and the arts and possessed a strong character. Her disciplined upbringing ensured she learned the virtues of efficiency, decency and order, which in turn were passed on to her children, influencing the young Reinhard to view his life in line with his mother's doctrines. Elisabeth believed she would inherit the famous Dresden Conservatoire after the death of her mother, but her two brothers, although unable to direct the school themselves through lack of skill, saw the institution as a source of income, and insisted on their two-thirds share; their years of study as merchants in London had not been wasted.

Following their marriage, the happy couple moved to Halle, where Bruno had founded his own academy of music. Although insignificant compared to his in-laws' world famous conservatoire, Bruno had hopes of improvement. It was obvious to him that he would one day be the director of the Dresden school. Who else had the musical talent and experience? They both viewed the Halle academy as a temporary measure, but good grounding for their future role. Elisabeth encouraged her husband in the idea to establish their own school, prompted by her father. Bruno composed the prospectus for his school: *"After marriage into a pedagogic family, in December 1897 (his wife is the daughter of his former teacher, Professor Krantz), Heydrich also became a teacher, through the encouragement and instruction of the latter"* [1]. Sadly, their ambition in Dresden was never realised, and this powerful disappointment stayed with Elisabeth for the rest of her life; however they both settled to make the most of their situation.

Bruno was never interested in the administrative and financial aspects of running a school, and left this to his wife, while he concentrated on lessons in instruments, singing and composition. Elisabeth also taught pianoforte, which as the first of it's kind in Halle, saw enrolments for the school grow quickly, along with an enhanced reputation for success. In 1901, the school officially became a conservatoire. A musical education was fashionable at the time and in the provincial town of Halle a conservatoire was something of a novelty.

With the success of the school came acceptance by the 'higher society' within the town. Bruno counted the mayor among his associates and appearances at the local theatre increased his standing in the local community. He applied for recognition by the State Governor in Merseburg by way of a state charter in 1903 which although well recommended by the Halle Schools Committee, did not materialise until three years later. Bruno's name was also to be found on the membership lists of several of the town's musical societies, and he was also a founder member of the Schlaraffia Lodge, an organisation later suspected of freemasonry by his son's 'Sicherheitsdienst' (Security service). The title 'Professor of Music' was another ambition of the up and coming director of Halle's conservatoire, but this also was to prove elusive for the hard working father of the future chief of Hitler's Security Services.

The Heydrichs had already been blessed with a girl in 1901, who they named Maria, after her mother's second name. The sound of music students' renditions heralded the arrival of the new baby boy at ten-thirty in the morning of Monday 7th March 1904. Five days later, his father proudly registered the birth in the town register under entry number 669 [2]. Reinhard was to be followed by another boy, Heinz Siegfried, born eighteen months later.

During the summer of Reinhard's first year, the family and the conservatoire moved to new premises at Poststrasse 21. The success of the business was reflected in the size and central location of the new building; a four storey affair with the living quarters on the upper floors. Students in the classrooms below cannot have failed to hear the cries of the new infant mingling with the musical sounds of instruments and choristers. In 1906, the Heydrichs moved home again to yet more elegant premises at Gütchenstrasse 20.

The children had a rigid Catholic upbringing, (the results of their mother's beliefs and the fact that Bruno had converted to Catholicism from the Evangelical faith in order to marry Elisabeth). At times, Elszabeth's faith bordered on fanaticism which in later life was to bring her into conflict with Reinhard's vehement attitude towards the Church. The children's evening prayers were led by their mother and the family never failed to attend mass on Sundays. Elisabeth frequently resorted to corporal punishment, believing in the educational value of the stick.

Elisabeth was also responsible for the musical tutelage of the children, Bruno being occupied with the paying students. 'Little Reini', as Reinhard was affectionately known within the family, learnt to play piano, violin and the complexities of musical notation at an early age. By the time he started primary school at the age of six, he was found to be a gifted, intelligent child, unafraid of work, but a little introvert. Aspects of his later character are already discernible at this early stage of his life. A boyhood friend, Erich Schultze, ascertains that Reinhard Heydrich always seemed to be left out by the rest of the family, preferential treatment being afforded to his sister. This developed a tendency towards arrogance, brought about by his withdrawal into a world of his own. Other members of the family described him as a 'difficult child' who took after his mother's side.

In 1914, at the age of ten, Reinhard moved to the Reform Realgymnasium School in Friesenstrasse. This school specialised in the sciences, modern languages and history. Reinhard displayed a talent for chemistry and he decided that this would be his chosen career. He loved to experiment with different substances and often did so at home in private. It was during his period at this school that he discovered his competitive spirit, wishing to excel at everything he attempted, and experiencing disappointment when he failed to

Reinhard and his sister Maria

Bruno Heydrichs Konservatorium
für Musik und Theater

I. Hallesches Konservatorium

gegründet 1899

Halle a. d. Saale.

Auszüge aus dem Prospekt und den Satzungen (1907)
nebst Nachträgen (1918 und 1919).
Anmeldeschein.

Halle (Saale), den [illegible] März [illegible]

The prospectus for the Halle Conservatiore of music,
under the direction of Bruno Heydrich

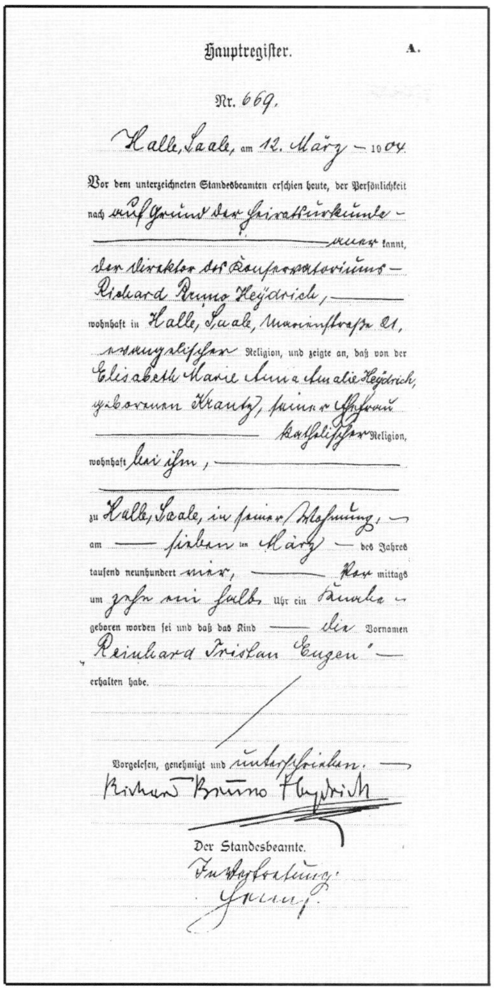

Hauptregister. A.

Nr. 669.

Halle, Saale, am 12. März 1904.

Vor dem unterzeichneten Standesbeamten erschien heute, der Persönlichkeit nach auf Grund der Heiratsurkunde anerkannt, der Direktor des Konservatoriums Richard Bruno Heydrich, wohnhaft in Halle, Saale, Marienstraße 21, evangelischer Religion, und zeigte an, daß von der Elisabeth Marie Anna Amalie Heydrich, geborenen Krantz, seiner Ehefrau, katholischer Religion, wohnhaft bei ihm, zu Halle, Saale, in seiner Wohnung, am siebten März des Jahres tausend neunhundert vier, vor mittags um zehn ein halb Uhr ein Knabe geboren worden sei und daß das Kind die Vornamen Reinhard Tristan Eugen erhalten habe.

Vorgelesen, genehmigt und unterschrieben.

Richard Bruno Heydrich

Der Standesbeamte.

In Vertretung.

Above: Probsteikirche on Mauerstrasse, Halle where the newborn Reinhard was baptised.

Above: Entry in the Halle birth register for Reinhard Heydrich dated 12th March 1904.

Right: Newspaper announcement of the new Heydrich arrival.

Mittwoch Abends 8½ Uhr Sitzung und Uebung Breitestraße 19, p.

Jahn'scher Turnverein.

Mittwoch u. Sonnabend Abend Turnübung in der Turnhalle am Roßplatz. Der Vorstand.

Dauerhafte Waschsäcke empfiehlt R. Katsch, Albrechtstr. 23.

Umtausch bis 15 April gestattet.

Confirmations-

Witwe Wille, Wansleben a. See.

Warnung. Ich warne hiermit jedermann, meiner Tochter Anna Berglen auf meinen Namen etwas zu borgen, da ich keine Zahlung leiste. Rudolph Berglen, Landsstädt.

Familien-Nachrichten.

Statt besonderer Meldung! Die glückliche Geburt eines überaus kraftvollen, gesunden Jungen zeigen hocherfreut an Bruno Heydrich und Frau Elisabeth geb. Krantz. Halle a. S., den 7. März 1904.

Für die vielen Beweise inniger Teilnahme und die reichen Kranzspenden bei dem Begräbnisse unserer lieben Mutter, Schwieger- und Großmutter, Frau Friederike Tempel, sagen wir allen unseren Verwandten, Freunden und Bekannten statt besonderer Meldung unseren herzlichsten Dank. Cöllme, Löbejün, Gottnau. Die trauernden Hinterbliebenen.

Above: A shopping centre built in the 1980's now occupys the site where Reinhard Heydrich was born.

Looking up Gütchenstrasse, the Heydrichs moved to number 20 in 1906.

The Heydrich family home in Poststrasse, Halle

The rear of Gütchenstrasse 20
Although this photograph was taken in 1997, the house remained unchanged since the 1940's

Heydrich's school in Halle

achieve his target. There is the well known story of Reinhard achieving a mark of 'good' instead of his usual 'very good' for a test paper in chemistry, he complained to his teacher and was punished for his attitude, but he did not shrink from his conviction that he deserved the higher mark [3]. He also developed an awareness of courage and tenacity, on one occasion climbing to the roof of the school to exhibit his nerve.

The young Reinhard also found himself to be the object of jibes by the other boys, unfortunately his voice was unusually high and this gave rise to the nickname 'goat'. He was looked upon by some as a weakling and received the obligatory beatings from the school bullies, however, a further nickname intimating him to be a Jew, caused him even greater pain.

Reinhard's father had always been a jolly fellow, seizing every opportunity to be the joker in company. He had found that his jocular impersonations of Jews were received with great enthusiasm. So much so that a rumour began to circulate that he was too good at his joking not to be Jewish himself and as a result his young sons became the object of ridicule. 'Isi, Isi', was the cry behind the young Heydrich boys and this only stopped when Heinz produced a knife and threatened those responsible. The family went to great lengths to deny these allegations, but they were never successful in totally dispelling the rumour. In 1926, Heinz was refused entry to a student union on the mistaken grounds that he was a Jew.

The events occurring throughout Europe could not fail to influence the youth of Germany and Reinhard was no exception. The Kaiser's Reich had always instilled a military awareness in the minds of the young men of the time and, with the outbreak of hostilities in August 1914, this became extreme. Mere mention of defeat was unthinkable, and the Heydrich family awaited the inevitable victory against the inferior armies of their country's enemies. As the war dragged on from months into years, Bruno Heydrich never wavered in his belief in victory, even in the last months of the war, he would write articles for publication concerning the forthcoming triumph. His sons also held their father's steadfast belief in the expected victorious outcome.

Meanwhile, Reinhard had struck up a friendship with one Erich Schultze, a boy four years his senior. He spent many a happy holiday with the Schultze family in their house at Wöllnau. The two boys decided to try and converse with the Russian prisoners of war working on the farm, spending their pocket money on Russian phrase books in order to learn the language. They also learned French, attaining an acceptable standard in both tongues.

Everything looked well for the fourteen year old Reinhard Heydrich when sudden disaster struck his world; following a long stalemate in the trenches, the German populace were becoming more disenchanted with the war and even the German Navy in Kiel suffered a sailors' mutiny. The workers had had enough, and Wilhelm II was forced to abdicate his throne. An armistice was signed by representatives of the new government and the unbelievable happened;in 1918 Germany was defeated. Political unrest spread throughout Germany and even reached the bourgeois citizens of Halle. Inflation rocketed, badly affecting small businesses, including that of the Heydrich family. Communists and anarchists roamed the countryside and towns, imposing their will and street fighting became common.

As a result of the inflationary measures of the new government, Bruno was forced to write what amounted to a begging letter to the Mayor of Halle, informing him that the conservatoire was about to go into liquidation. Although their position was to later improve, the Heydrichs never recovered their previous standing. All this made a strong impact on Reinhard Heydrich; for the first time, he became involved in politics.

Reinhard Heydrich, along with the rest of the upper school of the Reform Realgymnasium, joined the Halle volunteer corps [4]. This was a civil defence corps responsible to General Märker. A Technische Nothilfe membership card from around this time displays a photograph of a very young looking Heydrich with a rather youthful signature, not yet developed into the more familiar angular handwriting of later years. In a 1937 questionnaire completed for his SS file, Heydrich states that from 1919 to 1920 he was a member of the 'Märker Freikorps' and that from1920 until 1922 he had belonged to the 'Deutschvölkischen Schutz- und Trutzbund' (Offensive and Defensive League of the German People) [5]. He had entered the world of politics, a move that would affect the rest of his life. There was, however, another influence that would also guide his destiny.

Obverse

Reverse

A young Heydrich's 'Technische Nothilfe' membership pass. At the time he was still living with his parents at Gütschenstrasse 20

Deutliche Schrift! — Rückgabetermin: 20. August 1937

Fragebogen

zur Ergänzung bzw. Berichtigung der Führerkartei und der Dienstaltersliste

Name und Vorname: Heydrich, Reinhard — Dienstgrad und SS-Nr.: SS-Gruppenführer, Nr.10.120

Parteinummer mit Eintrittsdatum **laut Parteibuch**: Nr.544.916, eingetreten am 1.5.1931

Falls außerhalb der deutschen Staatsgrenzen geboren, besaßen Sie eine fremde Staatsangehörigkeit? ---

Welche? ---

Einbürgerungsdatum laut Urkunde: ----

Hauptamtlicher SS-Führer? ja — Dienststellung und Einheit: Chef des Sicherheitshauptamtes d.RfSS, Chef der Sicherheitspolizei, Leiter des Geheimen Staatspolizeiamtes, Leiter des Reichskriminalpolizeiamtes

Verlobt: 24.12.1930 — verheiratet: 26.12.1931 — verwitwet: --- — geschieden: ---
(Beantwortung durch Datumseintragung)

Mädchenname der Verlobten bzw. der Frau (Name und Vorname): v.Osten, Lina, Mathilde

Geburtstag: 14.6.1911 — Geburtsort: Avendorf auf Fehmarn

Parteigenossin, NSF, NSV, FW? Pgn. 1.201.380, NSV.1.976.381
(mit jeweiliger Angabe der Mitgliedsnummer)

Geburtsdaten der Söhne: Klaus: 17.6.1933 zu Berlin, Heider: 28.12.1934 zu Berlin
(Stiefsöhne mit vorgesetztem »St«, Adoptiv- mit »A« und Pflegesöhne mit »P« bezeichnen)

Geburtsdaten der Töchter: ----
(Stieftöchter mit vorgesetztem »St«, Adoptiv- mit »A« und Pflegetöchter mit »P« bezeichnen)

Besuchen Ihre Söhne eine nationalpolitische Erziehungsanstalt? ----
(Sohn oder Söhne mit Geburtsdatumsangabe eintragen)

Welche? ---

Nur für nichthauptamtliche SS-Führer: Ihr jetziger Beruf:
(mit Angabe der Dienststellung)

Arbeitgeber:
(mit Angabe der Dienststelle und Ort)

Sind Sie evangelischer — katholischer Konfession oder gottgläubig?
(Zutreffendes unterstreichen)

Militärische Übungen **nach dem** 16. 3. 35 ---

a) Zeit: vom ... bis ... b) Truppenteil: ... c) Erreichter Dienstgrad:

d) Sind Sie im Besitz einer Kriegsbeorderung? nein
(Nur mit ja oder nein zu beantworten)

Kraftfahrzeugführer- und ~~Fahrlehrerscheine~~: XXXXXXXXXX 1 und 2 und Führerschein Seefahrt

Flugzeugführerscheine: A/2.

Zugehörigkeit zu (mit Zeitangabe von — bis): Deutschvölkischen Schutz-und Trutzbund 1920/22

Freikorps (Name): Märker, Halle u. Freikorps Halle — vom 1919 bis 1920, HJ vom ... bis ...

Stahlhelm vom ... bis ..., SA vom ... bis ...

Jungdo vom ... bis ..., NSKK vom ... bis ...

Sonstige Angaben: Pr.Staatsrat, M.d.R.
(z. B. Staatsrat, Ratsherr, Senator, Redner, Politischer Leiter, in der Bauernschaft, Reichsnährstand, Jägerei usw.)

Mitglied des Vereins »Lebensborn«? ja — Im Besitz des Julleuchters? ja

Ehrenzeichen der Bewegung: ---
(Goldenes Parteiabzeichen, Gauehrenzeichen, Coburger, Blutorden, Goldenes HJ-Abzeichen)

Olympia-Ehrenzeichen: 1. Klasse.
(Angabe der Klasse)

Sportabzeichen: SA Bronze — Reiter Silber — Reichs Silber — DLRG ---
(mit jeweiliger Angabe ob Bronze, Silber oder Gold)

Vor dem Feinde erworbene Auszeichnungen (mit ja oder nein beantworten) nein

1. Pour le mérite:
2. Goldenes preußisches Militärverdienstkreuz: (höchste Auszeichnung für den Unteroffiziers-Dienstgrad)
3. EK I:
4. EK II:
5. EK II am weißen Bande:
6. Ehrenkreuz für Frontkämpfer:
7. Sonstige im Felde erworbenen Landesorden:
8. Verwundetenabzeichen: (Eintragen, ob Schwarz, Silber oder Gold)

Irrtümer in der Dienstaltersliste vom 1. 12. 36, die die eigene Person betreffen, mitteilen:

Berlin SW.11, Prinz Albrecht Str.8., den 26.11.1937
(Ort) (Straße und Nummer) (Datum) (Unterschrift)

16.11.37.

Die Dienstaltersliste 1937 mit dem Stand vom 1. 12. wird kurz vor Weihnachten 1937 erscheinen. Bestellkarten gehen den Führern rechtzeitig zu.

4213 37 II D — Din 476 A 4

Heydrich's 1937 Fragebogen (Questionnaire)

Heydrich's questionnaire illustrates his first documented involvement in politics. He declares his membership of the 'Märker Freikorps' from 1919-1920 and the 'Deutsch völkischen Schutz-und Trutzbund' 1920-1922.

CHAPTER 2
A NAVAL CAREER

Admiral Graf von Luckner
He wrote the famous book
"The Sea Devil"

Reinhard Heydrich had long grown out of his desire to become a chemist, war and its after effects had changed his ambitions. Witnessing the manoeuvres of the German Navy while on holiday at Swinemunde left him with a feeling of unequalled pride, furthermore visits by an old friend of the family, Admiral Graf von Luckner, during which he related tales of naval adventure, fired the enthusiasm of the impressionable Heydrich. Von Luckner's famous book 'The Sea Devil' had pride of place on the young man's bookshelf. He regularly attended meeting halls, packed with the youth of Halle, to hear lectures by the admiral who had the status of a folk hero. All this made a profound impression on Heydrich who was determined to emulate his hero and become a famous admiral himself.

Elisabeth and Bruno had already decided that a musical career was ideal for their elder son, whose expert renditions on the violin were a testament to their tuition. It was a forgone conclusion in the Heydrich household that musical success awaited him, and so it was with disbelief they heard the news that their budding maestro had decided on an alternative military career. Arguments were raised on both sides, but it became obvious that their son was unshakeable in his resolve. The ever status-conscious Elisabeth considered a naval officer to be acceptable for the family prestige and Bruno realised that this would provide a secure income as after ten years, an officer was guarantied a pension. Reluctantly they agreed and the nervous Reinhard Heydrich reported for his initial training at Kiel-Holtenau on 30th March 1922, in possession of a present from his father, a black case containing his violin [1].

The new recruit joined Crew 22 in the second squad [2]. His first period of initial training was spent in Kiel which proved to be a difficult time due in part to his physical appearance. He was tall, over six feet, with narrow hips (later described as 'rather feminine' by Schellenberg), with sharp features, light blue eyes, a pink complexion and soft, white blond hair. Unfortunately, his falsetto voice had not deserted him with the onset of manhood. Considered too soft by his fellow crew members, he quickly received the nickname 'billy-goat'. It wasn't long before other names followed: 'heavenly goat' (a reference to his musical talents), 'blond Siegfried' and 'Moses Handel', another indication that he had not shed the stigma of his father's supposed Jewish ancestry. Once again, he reverted to solitude, avoiding contact with his comrades unless absolutely necessary and concentrating on his swimming, running and fencing.

Reinhard Heydrich's widow, Lina, relates the story of one particularly nasty character amongst the instructors. A short, fat, Polish man from West Prussia, took great delight in bullying the recruits, and in particular, the sensitive Heydrich. The instructor had a habit of encouraging the young men under his charge to display their courage by falling flat on their faces from the kneeling position with hands behind their backs. His enlarged stomach prevented any discomfort, but the younger men fell onto their unprotected heads. The bony Heydrich dreaded this painful manoeuvre. Off duty, the instructor also picked upon the somewhat delicate youth from Halle; after consuming large quantities of alcohol, he would summon the young recruit from his sleep and order him to play a sentimental tune on his violin. The instructor was particularly fond of the Toselli Serenade, Heydrich never forgot that piece of music, always taking great pains to switch it off when he heard it played on the radio. Later Heydrich would also take 'an informed interest' in the 'little, fat, roundheaded racial types of the East' [3].

After completing his basic training, Heydrich was posted to the 'Braunschweig' [4]. Still a loner, he now encountered his first taste of the Navy's code of honour. During a period of leave, he visited his hometown and was spotted by an old adversary who taunted him with the phrase, *"Just look at the yid 'Süss' in his naval uniform."* This incident was relayed back to his comrades who enquired as to what his retaliation had consisted of. Heydrich is supposed to have replied, *"What should I have done?"* this indicated that he had taken no action, which was totally unacceptable to his colleagues, they promptly shunned him. He next spent three months aboard the training ship 'Niobe', where he developed a passion for sailing and on 1st July 1923, joined the crew of the cruiser 'Berlin'.

The commanding officer of the 'Berlin', Captain Wilfried von Löwenfeld, ran a harsh regime. This suited the still impressionable young Heydrich, who believed that only strict discipline could result in an above average crew, however, not all the ship's officers were of the same opinion. The executive officer, Lieutenant Commander Wilhelm Canaris, considered the captain's treatment of the cadets a little too severe.

Canaris had served aboard the 'Dresden' during the First World War and was a member of the ship's crew when she was blockaded in 1915 in the Magellan Straits by the British ship 'HMS Glasgow'. With no hope of escape, she was scuttled. Disguised as a Chilean subject, Lieutenant Canaris managed to evade the blockade in a Dutch vessel bound for Europe, even calling at Falmouth on route. Once back in the Fatherland, he became embroiled in the world of espionage, receiving a posting to neutral Madrid as an intelligence officer [5]. With such an adventurious and experienced background, the young cadets could not have failed to look upon their executive officer as anything other than a hero, none more so than Reinhard Heydrich. His widow, Lina, acknowledges that Canaris made a profound impression on her husband.....*"Heinrich Himmler played a decisive part in Reinhard's life. Only Wilhelm Canaris, head of German military intelligence, had an equally fateful influence on him"* [6].

Wilhelm Canaris

Erika, the gentle wife of Canaris, played the violin and held musical evenings at their home on Sundays (favouring compositions by Mozart and Haydn), a vacancy came up for a second violin in her string quartet. Aware of Heydrich's musical talent, Canaris invited him to attend one evening; Erika enthused over the young man's sensitive playing and he soon became a regular guest. Tales of Canaris' exploits during his time in the intelligence service must have also made an impression on the young Heydrich, which would ironically be useful later in his life. Heydrich took full advantage of this unprecedented situation as a house guest of one of his commanders, and mixed with other society families in Kiel. During this time he joined a private fencing club and also bought a motorcycle.

On 1st April 1924, Heydrich was promoted to Midshipman, serving at the Marineschule Mürwick as a member of Crew 22, until 1925. During that year, he underwent training in weaponry and spent his off-duty time sailing, fencing, swimming and horse riding, (breaking his nose in a riding accident at the Army Sports School at Wünsdorf) [7]. His next posting, from January to September 1926, was aboard the 'Braunschweig', he was now a Senior Midshipman, and this was followed by service on the Admiral's flagship, 'Schleswig-Holstein'. On 1st October 1926, Heydrich was promoted to Sub-Lieutenant and subsequently trained as a radio and signals officer. According to Wighton, having obtained his navigation certificate, Heydrich apparently served for a short period as the adjutant of the forerunner of the German naval motor-torpedo squadron, the Schnellbootverband, in Wilhelmshaven [8].

With promotion came greater freedom and flexibility to use his spare time. Heydrich concentrated on his physical fitness, spending many hours at the shooting range and becoming a member of the Navy pentathlon team. Later in 1928, he was chosen to represent his service, however, he failed to achieve his hoped for results, being placed third behind two army representatives. Fencing also played a major part in Heydrich's life, in 1927 he became a member of a team of four at the Second German Officers' Fencing Tournament in Dresden. Eliminated in the preliminary rounds and much to the annoyance and embarrassment of his fellow team members, Heydrich flung his rapier to the floor in disgust after his final defeat [9]. Nothing but perfection would ever satisfy him. This was also true in his study of Russian, English and French languages.

Heydrich was further promoted in 1928 to the rank of First Lieutenant and another transfer, this time to the Admiral's Division of the Baltic naval station in Kiel, as a communications officer. Calic describes this posting as that of an intelligence officer and states his former colleagues noticed an abrupt change in the new lieutenant, who apparently wished to keep his comrades at a distance. Suggesting that Heydrich was concerned over his sensitive posting in a secret base, Calic would have us believe that he did not trust his fellow naval officers, but did not mind acting as a sort of Casanova in the presence of women, mixing with them freely and making love when the situation arose. Are we to accept that Heydrich was *that* stupid? There is no doubt that the young officer was attracted to young women, as are most men of his age, but to suggest that he was free with his conversations with them, when he feared a slip of his tongue with his comrades seems unlikely. Calic also stresses throughout his book that Heydrich was a staunch supporter of Hitler, holding powerful political views during his naval service. To date there is no evidence to support this view, on the contrary, Lina states in her post-war autobiography that the young Reinhard Heydrich had

A view of Kiel-Holtenau, where the young Heydrich reported for initial training in March 1922.

The naval academy in Kiel.

Marineschule Mürwick

The main training school for future German naval officers.

A typical quarters occupied by a student such as Heydrich.

The students' mess

The main hall

The Academy dining room

The Crew 22 at Marineschule Mürwick. This photograph was taken in 1924 after Heydrich was promoted to Midshipman. Heydrich stands at position '48' (an enlargement of him is shown upper left).

Namensliste

1. St.Zahlm.Rawengel
2. St.Arzt Dr.Lohmeyer
3. Kptl. Warzecha
4. Kaptl.(Ing) Ventzlaff
5. Rittm. Bernhard
6. Ob.St.Arzt Dr. Pillet
7. Freg.Kpt. Kopp
8. Kapt.z.S. Tilleßen
9. K.Kpt. v. Bredow
10. Kptl. Weißbach
11. M.Baurat Schotte
12. Kptl. Witschetzky
13. Kptl. Andriano
14. Kptl.(Ing) Ziege[illegible]
15. Wegener
16. Oblt.Z.S. Kay
17. Ass.Arzt Dr.Kubitzki
18. Kptl. v.Treskow
19. Oblt.Z.S.Schönermark
20. Oblt.z.S. Bonte
21. Lt.(Ing) Liebhard
22. Oblt.z.S. Fricke
23. Oblt.z.S. Rollmann
24. Ob.Zahlm. Sieh
25. Edmund Bey
26. Lehmann
27. Graser
28. Max Becker
29. Rehm
30. Bauer
31. Fuhrke
32. Hamkens
33. Mettig
34. Otto
35. v.Brosy-Steinberg
36. Kaempf
37. Gynzel
38. Magdalinski
39. Nimz
40. Trüdinger
41. Minner
42. Stellmacher
43. Rothe
44. Schall
45. Junge
46. Hinrichs
47. Schuldt
48. Heydrich
49. Kähler
50. Schneider
51. Reinicke
52. Meisner
53. Baustaedt
54. Knuth
55. Strauch
56. Erdmenger
57. Bernt
58. Nötzold
59. Heerhartz
60. Baumann
61. Rechel
62. Albrecht
63. Grunwald
64. Deters
65. Hülsemann
66. Brachmann
67. v.Wangenheim
68. Assmann
69. Dobratz
70. Girscher
71. Günther
72. Schmidt,Moritz
73. Lebram
74. Thilo
75. Smidt
76. Nettelbek
77. Stockmann
78. Beucke
79. Dyckerhoff
80. Jasper
81. Blaesle
82. Fuchs.
83. Bachmann

The complete name list of those with Crew 22, Heydrich is numbered 48 which relates to the numbering of the proceeding photograph.

Above: The crew of the 'Braunschweig' ; this was Heydrich's first sea posting.

Right: The Admiral's flagship 'Schleswig-Holstein'.

48 Anwärter für die Seeoffizierlaufbahn. — Ingenieuroffiziere der Marine.

1922

Schmidt [30. 1. 03]	M. Sch. Flensburg-Mürwik, z. Zt. Niobe, später Berlin	O	1. 4.23
Nimz [10. 2. 02]	desgl.	O	1. 4.23
Schneider [10. 3. 04]	desgl.	O	1. 4.23
Ollrogge [16. 10. 03]	desgl.	O	1. 4.23
Thilo [4. 1. 03]	desgl.	O	1. 4.23
Jasper [17. 5. 02]	desgl.	O	1. 4.23
Knuth [23. 1. 04]	desgl.	O	1. 4.23
Beucke [12. 1. 04]	desgl.	O	1. 4.23
Schuldt [14. 6. 01]	desgl.	O	1. 4.23
Girscher [16. 2. 01]	desgl.	O	1. 4.23
Bauer [24. 2. 01]	desgl.	O	1. 4.23
Ginzel [27. 9. 01]	desgl.	O	1. 4.23
Baumann [20. 3. 03]	desgl.	O	1. 4.23
Rehm [22. 12. 03]	desgl.	O	1. 4.23
Rechel [1. 12. 02]	desgl.	O	1. 4.23
Dnckerhoff [7. 11. 03]	desgl.	O	1. 4.23
Hinrichs [31. 1. 04]	desgl.	O	1. 4.23
Seutter von Lötzen [31. 12. 01]	desgl.	O	1. 4.23
Otto [28. 2. 02]	desgl.	O	1. 4.23
Heydrich [7. 3. 04]	desgl.	O	1. 4.23
Baustaedt [26. 7. 03]	desgl.	O	1. 4.23
Grunwald [27. 3. 03]	desgl.	O	1. 4.23
Bläßle [9. 11. 03]	desgl.	O	1. 4.23

Ingenieuroffiziere der Marine.

Kontreadmiral des Marineingenieurwesens.

1893.	Friedrich [10. 10. 74] ✠1 ✠ M. L., Ing. Offiz. b. Stabe	B	1. 4.23

Kapitäne zur See des Marineingenieurwesens.

1893.	Steinkopf [21. 6. 74] ✠1 ✠ St. Ing.	O	1. 4.22
	Hilbig [13. 12. 74] ✠1 ✠ St. Ing.	N	1. 4.23

Fregattenkapitäne des Marineingenieurwesens.

1893.	Köppen [1. 12. 73] ✠1 ✠ M. Archiv	B	1. 4.22
1894.	Jacks [22. 2. 73] ✠1 ✠ *SA3a✕ HH OFA1* B. J., Insp. Ing.	O	1. 4.22
	Rave [22. 5. 75] ✠1 ✠ *LübH* B. S. O., Verb. Ing.	O	1. 4.22
	Beyer [20. 5. 75] ✠1 ✠ *SA3a✕* M. L.	B	1. 4 23

Korvettenkapitäne des Marineingenieurwesens.

1895.	Kilb [26. 9. 71] ✠1 ✠ B. S. N., Verb. Ing.	N	1. 4.21
1896.	de la Sauce (Wilhelm) [23. 8. 78] ✠1 ✠ T. M. J., Insp. Ing.	O	1. 4 21
1897.	Berndt (Paul) [21. 3. 79] ✠1 ✠ M. L.	B	1. 7.21
	Heinze [6. 11. 78] ✠1 ✠ Kom. d. M. Sch. Kiel-Wik	N	1.10 21
	Stücker [20. 10. 77] ✠1 ✠ *HSME1 HH* M. Werft Wilhh., Assist. d. Ausrüst. u. Torp. Ress.	N	1. 2.22

Above: Naval listing showing Heydrich's posting on 1st April 1923 to the 'Niobe' and later the 'Berlin'.

14 Marinestation der Ostsee.

Intendant Schwarz, s. M. Int. Kiel.
M. Ob. Pfarrer Dehmel, Evang. St. Pfarrer.
„ Pfarrer Fenger.
„ Ob. Pfarrer Kräuter, Kath. St. Pfarrer.

M. Anwalt Reichard. | M. Anwalt Dr. Buchholz, s. Kdtr. Swinemünde.

Hafenkapitän Kiel
und
Marinekommissar für den Kaiser-Wilhelm-Kanal.

F. Kapt. Weisbach (Raimund), Kombt. von Kiel.

Stationsrechnungsamt.

Vorst.: M. Ob. Zahlm. Pila. | M. Zahlm. Liermann.

Zur Verfügung des Stationschefs:

Oblt. z. S. Geisse.
„ „ Ferber.
„ „ von Blessingh.
„ „ von Wild.
„ „ Hinrichs.
„ „ Hahn.
„ „ von Kamptz, später „Karlsruhe".
„ „ Schulz (Karl-Heinrich).

Lt. z. S. Zaubzer, später „Karlsruhe".
„ „ Schultz (Herbert), desgl.
Oblt. (Ing.) Born.
M. Ob. St. Arzt Dr. Kränz, k. z. Universität Freiburg i. Br.
„ St. Arzt Dr. Evers, k. z. Hygien. Institut München.
„ „ „ Dr. Möller, k. z. Universität
„ Ob. Zahlm. Seefeldt. [Kiel.

Marinenachrichtenoffiziere:

Kaptlt. Wiegner — Neumünster —, zugl. Kdtr. Kiel.
Oblt. z. S. Schröder (Willy) — Warnemünde —, zugl. II/S. D. O. (b. d. Standortält. Stralsund).
„ „ Manhenke — Flensburg-Mürwik —, zugl. T. N. S., K. Führ.
„ „ Bassenge — Pillau —, zugl. Kdtr. das.
„ „ Wolf (Alfred) — Kiel —, zugl. M. S. Friedrichsort (b. d. Standortält. das.).
„ „ Heydrich, N. A. d. St. O.
„ „ Lucan — Swinemünde —, zugl. Kdtr. das. u. m. W. d. G. d. M. N. O. Stolpmünde b.
„ „ Langheld, N. A. d. St. O.

Stationstender „Nordsee".
Kiel.
Kombt.: Lt. z. S. Krause (Otto).

Above: A page from the official German naval rank list from 5th November 1930, showing Heydrich as an Oberleutnant zu See, Marinenachrichtenoffiziere (Marine Signal Officer).

no strong views other than those of a nationalist, proud of his country and willing to defend it in his capacity as a serving member of the armed forces.

Heydrich was now established in both his rank and position in society, albeit still shy and uncomfortable in large gatherings, (a weakness in his character that would even stay with him in later years when in the high position of Acting Reichsprotektor). The prospect of further promotions loomed before him since he had received excellent reports from his superiors. His instructor in the naval radio college, the later Vice Admiral Gustav Kleikamp, wrote.... *"His talents, knowledge and ability have placed him well above average. Without doubt, this will be endorsed by many later superior officers "*[10]. His boyhood friend, Schultze, recalls.... *"We were all certain that he would go far in the Navy because of his ambition and his ability. He was never content...as a Lieutenant he was already dreaming of becoming an Admiral"* [11]. Meanwhile a young woman was about to enter his life.

A youthful Heydrich
in naval uniform

Lina Mathilde von Osten was eighteen years of age, blonde and beautiful from Avendorf on the Baltic island of Fehmarn. She was attending the 'Mädchenberufsschule' in Kiel, studying to be an engineering teacher and had lodgings at the Henriettenhaus in Kieler Kornerstrasse. Lina mentioned post-war that one evening in November 1930, she sat with three friends in Room 18 at the Henriettenhaus, entertaining them with caricatures of her aunts. The conversation turned to a ball given by the school rowing club, which was affiliated to the Schleswig-Holstein Sailing and Rowing Association, it was to be held in the music room on the 6th December. Lina was not keen to attend, but agreed to do so as an old friend, Wulf, had urged her to accompany him. Each class had been instructed to send one representative (and as a fellow student and friend had agreed to go, Lina reluctantly volunteered). Three days before the ball, Wulf sent his apologies and withdrew, the pressures of duty on his farm were too great. Lina also wanted to pull out, but her three friends encouraged her to go.

On the evening of the ball, Lina and her friend were dismayed to find that nearly all the participants were fellow female students and that they were in for a boring time. Lina was just about to leave when two young naval officers approached their group, and managed to manoeuvre two of the young women to join their table, Lina was one of the two. The dark haired, shorter of the two young men, introduced himself as von Manstein and Lina was trying to think of a formal introduction when the blond, taller of the two, said, *"Heydrich, Reinhard Heydrich"*. The attraction was immediate and Heydrich spent the remainder of the evening in her company, walking her home and requesting a further meeting. Lina also felt drawn to the shy young Heydrich and agreed to meet him two days later, they walked through the Hohenzollern Park and talked at length about themselves. Heydrich produced two tickets for the theatre the following evening and, after Lina had arranged to obtain the key to the Henriettenhaus, she met him again.

Heydrich arrived in his best full uniform and after the performance they went to Wicks Weinkeller in the Brunswick area, where they sat in silence, finally the silence was broken by the impetuous Heydrich proposing marriage. Taken aback she said, *"My God, Herr Heydrich, you know nothing about me and even less about my family. You don't even know who or what my father is. The Navy must have regulations about who their officers can marry"* [12]. Heydrich stated that this would not pose a problem and repeated his proposal, before leaving she agreed to marry him and they became secretly engaged on 18th December 1930, just twelve days after their first meeting. It was a relationship of love that would last for the rest of their lives and long after his death.

Lina wrote to her father, informing him of her decision and Heydrich received a welcome invitation to the von Osten home in Lütjenbrode as a guest for Christmas. He arrived with his violin and played for his future wife and parents-in-law. Lina was captivated by his gentle playing and said years after, *"I doubt if I would ever have married him had he not played the violin so beautifully"* [13]. Reinhard impressed his future father-in-law, the local school teacher, with his life story and his future plans in the Navy. The prospect of a naval officer in the family must also have held a certain appeal. Herr von Osten told Reinhard his family history, stating that he was the second son, (in a family of six boys and two girls), of a wealthy landowner from northern Germany. Being the second son, he had to give up all claims to the family farm and, in 1896, left Eckernförde for the island of Fehmarn, taking up a position as schoolteacher, where he met and married Lina's mother, 'Thilde' Hiss. She had been one of ten children whose father was a merchant and captain, the family having lived on the island for hundreds of years. After the First World War, they had fallen into poverty and moved to Lütjenbrode, in the red brick school house where they now lived [14].

Lina was worried that Heydrich was becoming bored, but he insisted on hearing more, wanting to know all about his new family. The von Ostens had celebrated their silver wedding anniversary on 18th October 1923 and, although von Osten admitted that he did not consider the Church as a world power, Lina had been confirmed in the village church at Grossenbrode. She had one brother, Jürgen, who was a follower of National Socialism after having heard Hitler speak in Eckernförde. Jürgen had joined the Party (NSDAP) and the para-military 'Sturmabteilung', or 'SA' as it was known, and spoke excitedly about the movement to his sister. Lina attended a rally in 1929 and subsequently joined herself, as Party member number 1201380 [15]. This may well have been Heydrich's first direct introduction to the National Socialist Party. It is interesting to note that Lina maintained that Heydrich never read "Mein Kampf", the NSDAP 'bible'.

According to Lina, Heydrich possessed little sense of the value of money and in fact had some debts when they first met. During Heydrich's naval service, unlike many of his colleagues, he never asked his mother to do his washing and ironing. His dirty clothes lay in the washtub and rather than do the chore himself, he would purchase new items. Lina states that she once discovered no less than 34 white uniform shirts, over 60 square collars and 107 handkerchiefs belonging to her Reinhard [16]. This small failing certainly did nothing to change Lina's passion for her new man, in fact they would soon be married.

The couple became officially engaged on Boxing Day 1930 and they spent the following days, until the New Year, discussing plans for the wedding. They wished the engagement to be short, but the marriage could not take place for some months, as Lina had to finish her matriculation examinations in March of 1931 (and Heydrich required permission from his superiors) [17]. The whole visit had been a total success with Heydrich fitting in well with the nationalist views of the von Osten family. With the onset of the New Year, Heydrich's leave came to an end and he returned to Kiel without Lina, whose holidays had not yet finished. Everything looked well for Lieutenant Reinhard Heydrich and he proudly announced his engagement publicly, hoping for a September wedding later that year.

At the end of her holidays, Lina boarded the train to Kiel and was met by a rather stunned looking fiancé at the main railway station. Sensing something was wrong, she asked what was troubling her man. Heydrich confessed that a problem had arisen with a young woman he had courted before meeting Lina. She was a pupil at the 'Kolonialfrauenschule' (Colonial Girls School) in Rendsburg and was now living with her parents in Potsdam. Her father was a dockyard superintendent on familiar terms with Admiral Raeder and was a man with a certain amount of influence in Berlin. He had met her at a sailing regatta ball and she visited him in Kiel. Without lodgings for the night, Heydrich insisted that she stay at his address, whereby he informed his landlady. Nothing untoward had happened, but she had assumed that a proposal of marriage was shortly to follow. On discovery of his engagement to another woman, she had suffered a breakdown. Lina was sceptical but understanding of his explanation, unfortunately for Heydrich, the girl's father was not so understanding, considering Heydrich's behaviour as disgraceful and not becoming that of a naval officer. He had attempted to make the Lieutenant see reason, but having failed, he lodged an official complaint with Heydrich's superiors in Berlin, citing his actions as dishonourable.

With the complaint lodged, a Court of Honour was convened, chaired by the commander of the Baltic naval station, Admiral Gottfried Hansen. Other officers included Gustav Kleikamp, Heydrich's old instructor. The proceedings were looked upon by Heydrich as rather foolish and he treated them with a certain amount of indifference, refusing to accept that his actions had been incorrect. This view was not shared by his peers who promptly sent their decision to Admiral Raeder for a ruling on the Lieutenant's future. At this stage, Heydrich's career had not been terminated, although his position was precarious. Raeder soon ruled that First Lieutenant Reinhard Heydrich was no longer suitable to wear the uniform and consequently he was dismissed from the service with a monthly payment of two hundred marks for two years [18].

Heydrich had not reached the required ten years service to qualify for a pension and reserve officers were forbidden by the Versailles Treaty of 1919, suddenly he was now unemployed with little or no prospects. Stunned by the decision, the ex-naval man travelled to Halle, accompanied by his fiancée, in order to break the news to his parents.

The Hohenzollernpark in Kiel where the young Reinhard and Lina had their first official date on 8th December 1930.

The Henriettenhaus in Kiel, Lina von Osten was lodging here at the time she met the young Lieutenant Heydrich.

The von Osten family home, Lina's bedroom was situated within the gable end on the viewers left. (photograph taken in 1997)

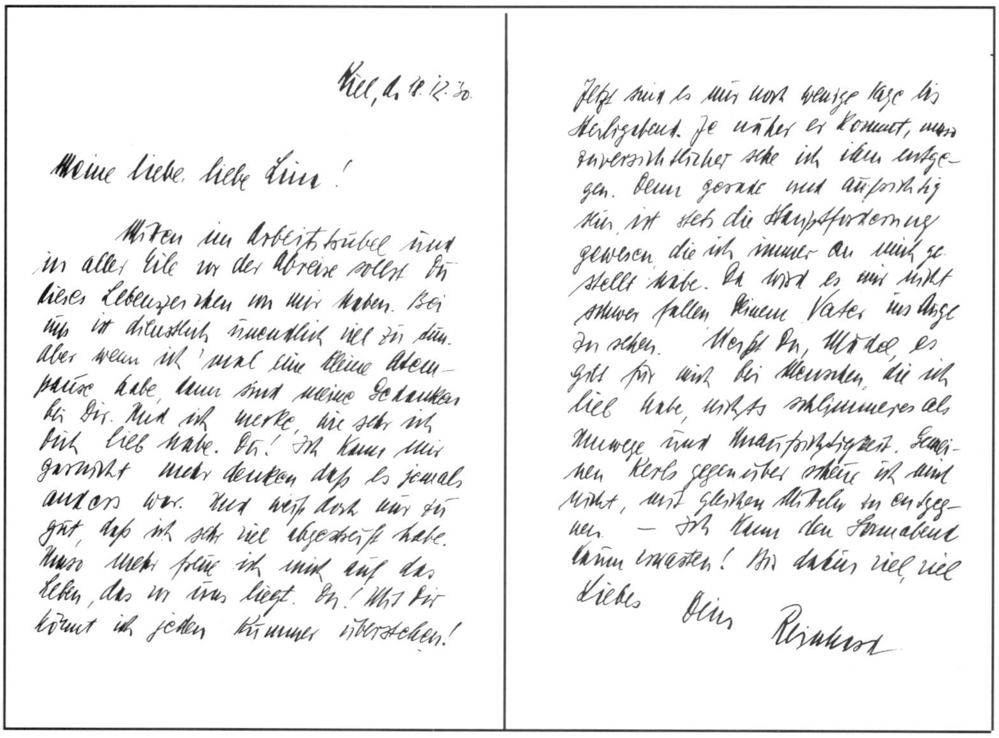

Kiel, d. 18.12.30.

Meine liebe, liebe Lina!

Mitten im Arbeitstrubel und in aller Eile vor der Abreise sollst Du dieses Lebenszeichen von mir haben. Bei uns ist dienstlich unendlich viel zu tun. Aber wenn ich 'mal eine kleine Atempause habe, dann sind meine Gedanken bei Dir. Und ich merke, wie sehr ich Dich lieb habe. Du! Ich kann mir garnicht mehr denken daß es jemals anders war. Und weiß doch nur zu gut, daß ich sehr viel abgeschlossen habe. Umso mehr freue ich mich auf das Leben, das vor uns liegt. Du! Mit Dir könnt ich jeden Kummer überstehen!

Jetzt sind es nur noch wenige Tage bis Heiligabend. Je näher er kommt, umso zuversichtlicher sehe ich ihm entgegen. Denn gerade und aufrichtig sein, ist stets die Hauptforderung gewesen, die ich immer an mich gestellt habe. Da wird es mir nicht schwer fallen Deinem Vater ins Auge zu sehen. Merkst Du, Mädel, es gibt für mich bei Menschen, die ich lieb habe, nichts schlimmeres als Umwege und Unaufrichtigkeit. Gemeinen Kerls gegenüber scheue ich mich nicht, mit gleichen Mitteln zu entgegnen. — Ich kann den Sonnabend kaum erwarten! Bis dahin viel viel Liebes

Dein Reinhard

Letter dated 18th December 1930 from Heydrich to Lina von Osten. This letter was written just three weeks after their engagement. Heydrich mentions that he is very busy at work and expresses his love for Lina. He is looking forward to their life together and Christmas Eve when he can *"look her father in the eye"*. This relates to when the couple intended to tell Lina's parents of their secret engagement Heydrich ends the letter by telling Lina that he dislikes indirectness and insincerity with people he loves.

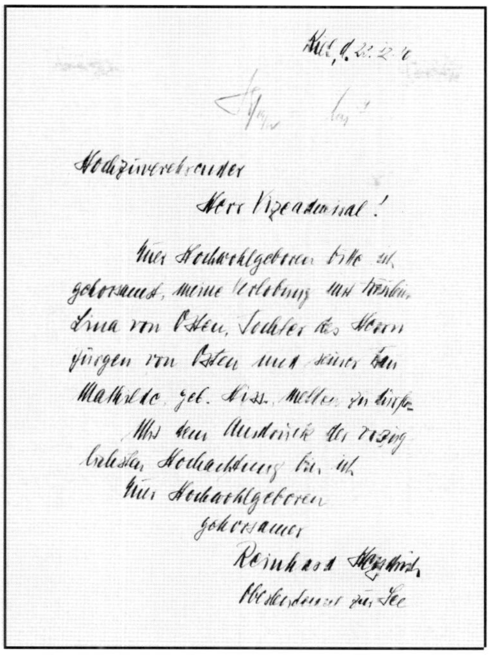

Kiel, d. 23.12.30

Hochzuverehrender
Herr Vizeadmiral!

Euer Hochwohlgeboren bitte ich gehorsamst, meine Verlobung mit Fräulein Lina von Osten, Tochter des Herrn Jürgen von Osten und seiner Frau Mathilde geb. Hiss, melden zu dürfen.
Mit dem Ausdruck der vorzüglichsten Hochachtung bin ich
Euer Hochwohlgeboren
gehorsamer
Reinhard Heydrich
Oberleutnant zur See

Heydrich's letter dated 23rd December 1930, to his commanding officer. The letter reads, 'Highly esteemed Vice-Admiral ! I beg to inform Your Honour of my engagement with Fräulein Lina von Osten, daughter of Jürgen von Osten and his wife Mathilde, born Hiss. With my expression of deep respect, I remain Your Honour's obediant Reinhard Heydrich - Oberleutnant zur See.

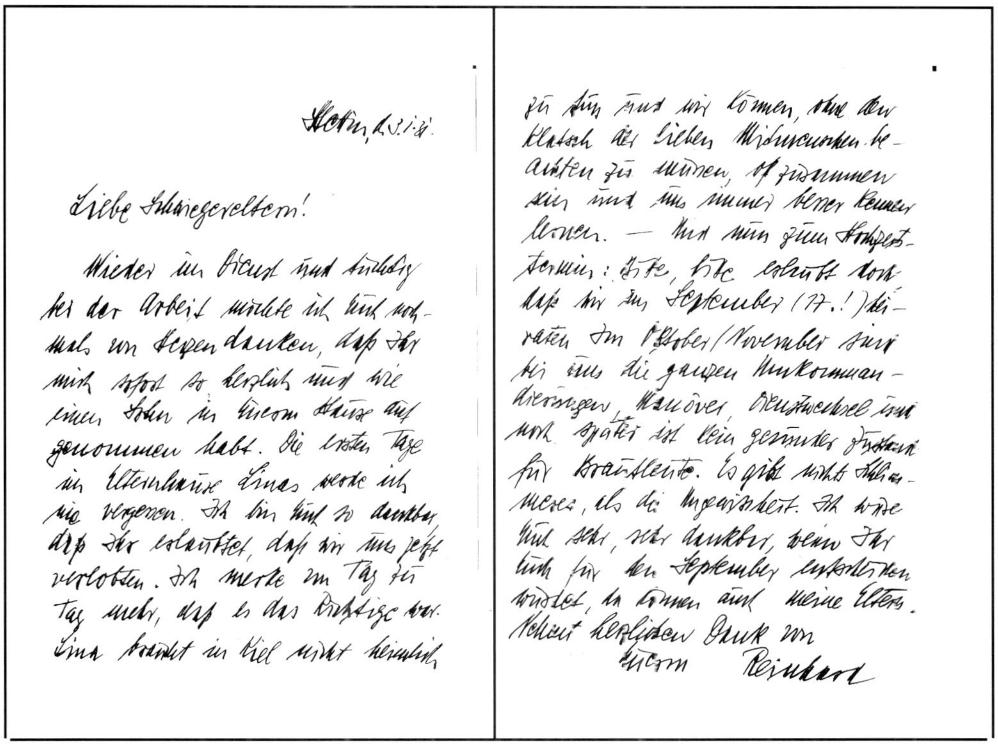

Stettin, d. 3.1.31.

Liebe Schwiegereltern!

Wieder im Dienst und tüchtig bei der Arbeit möchte ich Euch nochmals von Herzen danken, daß Ihr mich sofort so herzlich und wie einen Sohn in Euerem Hause aufgenommen habt. Die ersten Tage im Elternhause Linas werde ich nie vergessen. Ich bin Euch so dankbar, daß Ihr erlaubtet, daß wir uns jetzt verlobten. Ich merke von Tag zu Tag mehr, daß es das Richtige war. Lina braucht in Kiel nicht heimlich zu tun und wir können, ohne den Klatsch der lieben Mitmenschen beachten zu müssen, oft zusammen sein und uns immer besser kennen lernen. — Und nun zum Hochzeitstermin: bitte, bitte erlaubt doch daß wir im September (17.!) heiraten. Im Oktober/November sind bei uns die ganzen Unkommandierungen, Manöver, Dienstwechsel und noch später ist kein gesunder Zustand für Brautleute. Es gibt nichts Schlimmeres, als die Ungewissheit. Ich wäre Euch sehr, sehr dankbar, wenn Ihr Euch für den September entscheiden würdet, da können auch meine Eltern.
Nochmals herzlichen Dank von
Euerem Reinhard

Letter sent by Heydrich from Stettin on the 3rd January 1931,to his future parents-in-law informing them that he is working hard. Heydrich thanks them for treating him like a son (and mentions that he will never forget the first days he spent a their home with Lina) and for allowing the engagement and asks that the wedding date could be set for 17th September. Mention is made that his parents could make this date.

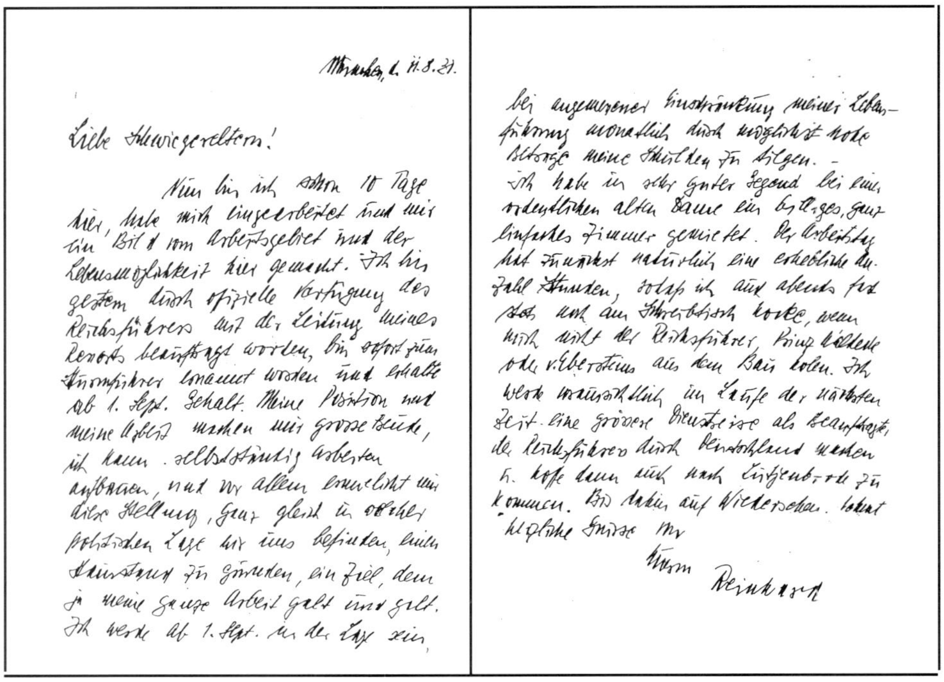

München, d. 11.8.31.

Liebe Schwiegereltern!

Nun bin ich schon 10 Tage hier, habe mich eingearbeitet und mir ein Bild vom Arbeitsgebiet und der Lebensmöglichkeit hier gemacht. Ich bin gestern durch offizielle Verfügung des Reichsführers mit der Leitung meines Referats beauftragt worden, bin sofort zum Sturmführer ernannt worden und erhalte ab 1. Sept. Gehalt. Meine Position und meine Arbeit machen mir grosse Freude, ich kann selbstständig arbeiten, aufbauen, und vor allem ermöglicht mir diese Stellung, ganz gleich in welcher politischen Lage wir uns befinden, einen Hausstand zu gründen, ein Ziel, dem ja meine ganze Arbeit galt und gilt. Ich werde ab 1. Sept. in der Lage sein, bei angemessener Einschränkung meiner Lebensführung monatlich durch möglichst hohe Beträge meine Schulden zu tilgen. – Ich habe in sehr guter Gegend bei einer ordentlichen alten Dame ein billiges, ganz einfaches Zimmer gemietet. Der Arbeitstag hat zunächst natürlich eine erhebliche Anzahl Stunden, sodass ich auch abends fest am Schreibtisch hocke, wenn mich nicht der Reichsführer, Prinz Waldeck oder v. Eberstein aus dem Bau holen. Ich werde wahrscheinlich im Laufe der nächsten Zeit eine grössere Dienstreise als Beauftragter des Reichsführers durch Deutschland machen und hoffe dann auch nach Lütjenbrode zu kommen. Bis dahin auf Wiedersehen. Recht herzliche Grüsse Ihr

Ihr Reinhard

Letter sent by Heydrich from Munich on the 11th August 1931,to his future parents-in-law after his dismissal from the navy. Heydrich has been in Munich for ten days and has settled into his new job within the SS. The day before he was promoted to SS-Sturmführer and ordered to take command of his department. Heydrich states that he will receive regular pay as from 1st September and can then start paying off his debts. A cheap and simple room has been rented from an old lady (Viktoria Edrich) in a nice area (Türkenstrasse 23). He works long hours and is always at his desk, often into the evening unless the RFSS, Prinz Waldeck or von Eberstein call him from the building. Heydrich finishes the letter by stating he may go on a trip through Germany as the RFSS representative and hopes he may able to visit them in Lütjenbrode.

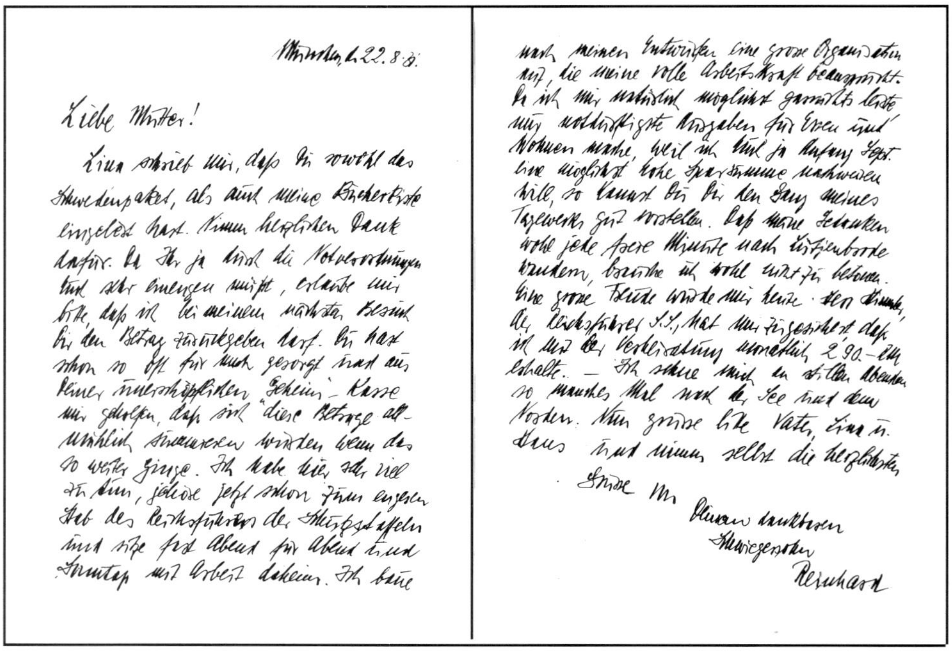

München, d. 22.8.31.

Liebe Mutter!

Lina schrieb mir, dass Sie sowohl das Schwedenpaket, als auch meine Bücherkiste eingelöst hat. Meinen herzlichen Dank dafür. Da Ihr ja durch die Notverordnungen und sehr einengen müsst, erlaube mir bitte, dass ich bei meinem nächsten Besuch Ihnen den Betrag zurückgeben darf. Sie hat schon so oft für mich gesorgt und aus ihrer unerschöpflichen „Geheim"-Kasse mir geholfen, dass sich "diese Beträge allmählich summieren würden, wenn das so weiter ginge. Ich habe hier sehr viel zu tun, gehöre jetzt schon zum engsten Stab des Reichsführers der Schutzstaffeln und sitze fast Abend für Abend und Sonntag mit Arbeit daheim. Ich baue nach meinen Entwürfen eine grosse Organisation auf, die meine volle Arbeitskraft beansprucht. Da ich mir natürlich möglichst genaueste Liste über notdürftigste Ausgaben für Essen und Wohnen mache, weil ich Euch ja Anfang Sept. eine möglichst hohe Sparsumme nachweisen will, so könnt Ihr Euch den Gang meines Tagewerks gut vorstellen. Dass meine Gedanken wohl jede freie Minute nach Lütjenbrode wandern, brauche ich wohl nicht zu betonen. Eine grosse Freude wurde mir heute im Dienst. Der Reichsführer S.S. hat mir zugesichert, dass ich mit der Verheiratung monatlich 290.- RM erhalte. – Ich sehne mich an stillen Abenden so manches Mal nach der See und dem Norden. Nun grüsse bitte Vater, Lina u. Hans und nimm selbst die herzlichsten Grüsse Ihr

Ihres dankbaren Schwiegersohns

Reinhard

Lettersent from Heydrich to Lina's mother on 22nd August 1931. He mentions that Lina has told him that Frau von Osten managed to redeem his belongings and his book. Heydrich thanks her and offers to repay her on his next visit. He is still very busy at work and now belongs to the closest staff of the RFSS, where he is developing a large organisation according to his own plans. Heydrich mentions that he only spends money on necessities, so that he can save and show Lina's parents that he can be economical. Good news has come from the RFSS, who has agreed to increase his salary to 290 RM a month from the point of Heydrich's wedding with Lina.

Admiral Raeder

Raeder decided to release Heydrich from naval service.

Admiral Hansen

Hansen was the Chairman of the Court of Honour

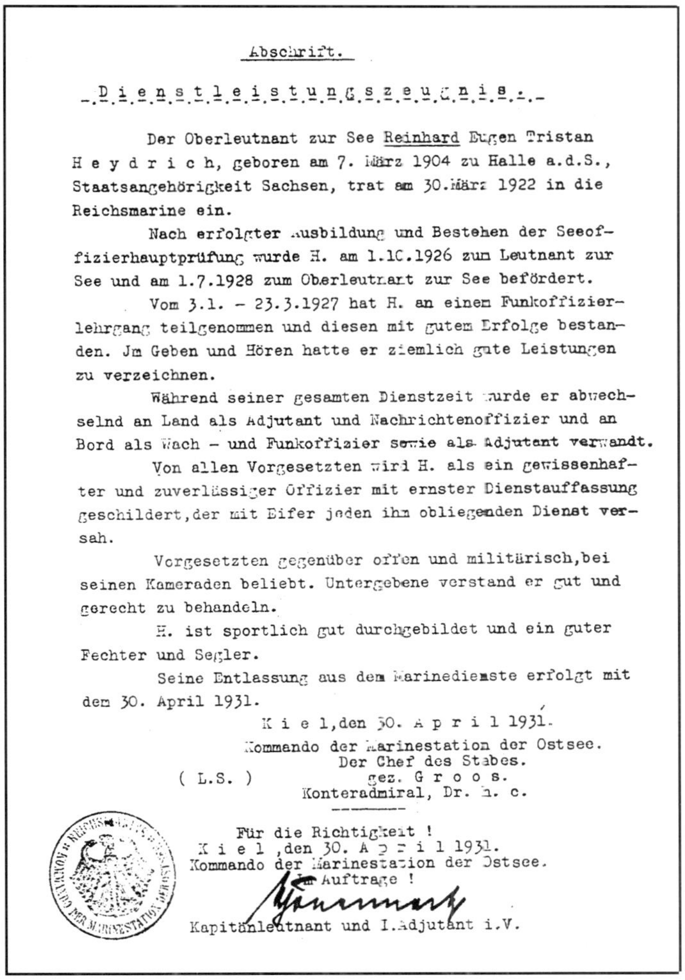

Abschrift.

D i e n s t l e i s t u n g s z e u g n i s .

Der Oberleutnant zur See Reinhard Eugen Tristan H e y d r i c h, geboren am 7. März 1904 zu Halle a.d.S., Staatsangehörigkeit Sachsen, trat am 30.März 1922 in die Reichsmarine ein.

Nach erfolgter Ausbildung und Bestehen der Seeoffizierhauptprüfung wurde H. am 1.10.1926 zum Leutnant zur See und am 1.7.1928 zum Oberleutnant zur See befördert.

Vom 3.1. - 23.3.1927 hat H. an einem Funkoffizierlehrgang teilgenommen und diesen mit gutem Erfolge bestanden. Jm Geben und Hören hatte er ziemlich gute Leistungen zu verzeichnen.

Während seiner gesamten Dienstzeit wurde er abwechselnd an Land als Adjutant und Nachrichtenoffizier und an Bord als Wach - und Funkoffizier sowie als Adjutant verwandt.

Von allen Vorgesetzten wird H. als ein gewissenhafter und zuverlässiger Offizier mit ernster Dienstauffassung geschildert, der mit Eifer jeden ihm obliegenden Dienst versah.

Vorgesetzten gegenüber offen und militärisch, bei seinen Kameraden beliebt. Untergebene verstand er gut und gerecht zu behandeln.

H. ist sportlich gut durchgebildet und ein guter Fechter und Segler.

Seine Entlassung aus dem Marinedienste erfolgt mit dem 30. April 1931.

K i e l, den 30. A p r i l 1931.
Kommando der Marinestation der Ostsee.
Der Chef des Stabes.
(L.S.) gez. G r o o s.
Konteradmiral, Dr. h. c.

Für die Richtigkeit !
K i e l, den 30. A p r i l 1931.
Kommando der Marinestation der Ostsee.
Im Auftrage !
Kapitänleutnant und I.Adjutant i.V.

Heydrich's termination report, which describes him as *"..a good sportsman, a good fencer and sailor"*.

Vice-Admiral Kleikamp

Kleikamp was Heydrich's instructor in the naval radio collegeand a member of the Court of Honour.

Admiral Groos

Groos was Chief-of-Staff at Marine Station Kiel and signed Heydrich's letter of termination.

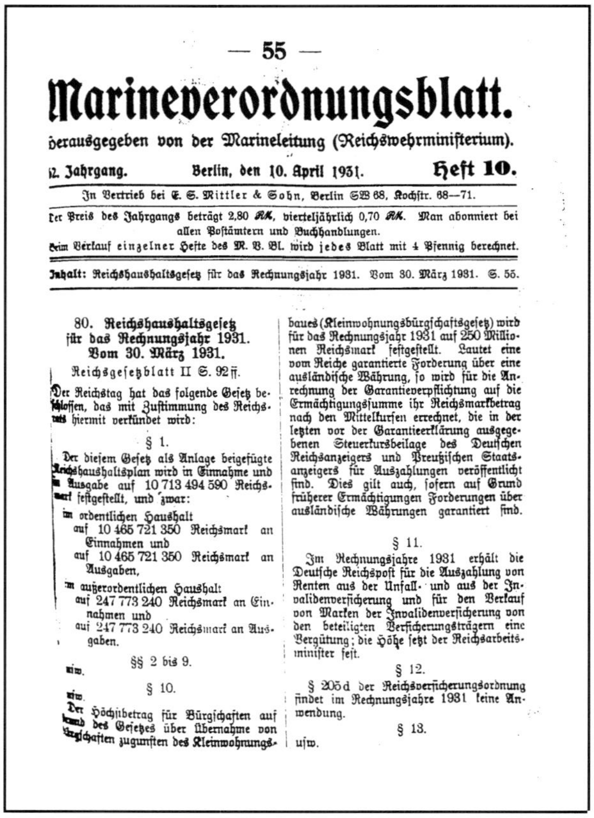

— 55 —

Marineverordnungsblatt.

Herausgegeben von der Marineleitung (Reichswehrministerium).

62. Jahrgang. Berlin, den 10. April 1931. Heft 10.

In Vertrieb bei E. S. Mittler & Sohn, Berlin SW 68, Kochstr. 68—71.

Der Preis des Jahrgangs beträgt 2,80 RM, vierteljährlich 0,70 RM. Man abonniert bei allen Postämtern und Buchhandlungen.

Beim Verkauf einzelner Hefte des M. V. Bl. wird jedes Blatt mit 4 Pfennig berechnet.

Inhalt: Reichshaushaltsgesetz für das Rechnungsjahr 1931. Vom 30. März 1931. S. 55.

80. **Reichshaushaltsgesetz für das Rechnungsjahr 1931. Vom 30. März 1931.**

Reichsgesetzblatt II S. 92ff.

Der Reichstag hat das folgende Gesetz beschlossen, das mit Zustimmung des Reichsrats hiermit verkündet wird:

§ 1.

Der diesem Gesetz als Anlage beigefügte Reichshaushaltsplan wird in Einnahme und in Ausgabe auf 10 713 494 590 Reichsmark festgestellt, und zwar:

im ordentlichen Haushalt
auf 10 465 721 350 Reichsmark an Einnahmen und
auf 10 465 721 350 Reichsmark an Ausgaben,

im außerordentlichen Haushalt
auf 247 773 240 Reichsmark an Einnahmen und
auf 247 773 240 Reichsmark an Ausgaben.

§§ 2 bis 9.

usw.

§ 10.

usw.

Der Höchstbetrag für Bürgschaften auf Grund des Gesetzes über Übernahme von Bürgschaften zugunsten des Kleinwohnungsbaues (Kleinwohnungsbürgschaftsgesetz) wird für das Rechnungsjahr 1931 auf 250 Millionen Reichsmark festgestellt. Lautet eine vom Reiche garantierte Forderung über eine ausländische Währung, so wird für die Anrechnung der Garantieverpflichtung auf die Ermächtigungssumme ihr Reichsmarkbetrag nach den Mittelkursen errechnet, die in der letzten vor der Garantieerklärung ausgegebenen Steuerkursbeilage des Deutschen Reichsanzeigers und Preußischen Staatsanzeigers für Auszahlungen veröffentlicht sind. Dies gilt auch, sofern auf Grund früherer Ermächtigungen Forderungen über ausländische Währungen garantiert sind.

§ 11.

Im Rechnungsjahre 1931 erhält die Deutsche Reichspost für die Auszahlung von Renten aus der Unfall- und aus der Invalidenversicherung und für den Verkauf von Marken der Invalidenversicherung von den beteiligten Versicherungsträgern eine Vergütung; die Höhe setzt der Reichsarbeitsminister fest.

§ 12.

§ 205d der Reichsversicherungsordnung findet im Rechnungsjahre 1931 keine Anwendung.

§ 13.

usw.

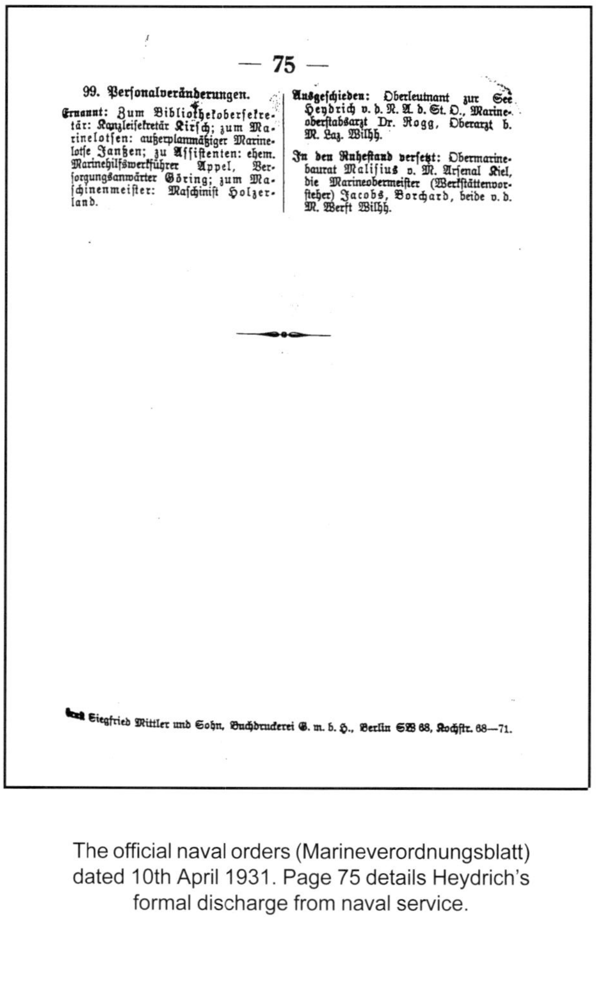

— 75 —

99. **Personalveränderungen.**

Ernannt: Zum Bibliothekobersekretär: Kanzleisekretär Kirsch; zum Marinelotsen: außerplanmäßiger Marinelotse Janßen; zu Assistenten: ehem. Marinehilfswerkführer Appel, Versorgungsanwärter Göring; zum Maschinenmeister: Maschinist Holzerland.

Ausgeschieden: Oberleutnant zur See Heydrich v. d. N. A. d. St. O., Marineoberstabsarzt Dr. Rogg, Oberarzt b. M. Laz. Wilhh.

In den Ruhestand versetzt: Obermarinebaurat Malisius v. M. Arsenal Kiel, die Marineobermeister (Werkstättenvorsteher) Jacobs, Borchard, beide v. d. M. Werft Wilhh.

Druck Siegfried Mittler und Sohn, Buchdruckerei G. m. b. H., Berlin SW 68, Kochstr. 68—71.

The official naval orders (Marineverordnungsblatt) dated 10th April 1931. Page 75 details Heydrich's formal discharge from naval service.

CHAPTER 3
A NEW DIRECTION

Elisabeth Heydrich was inconsolable, unable to believe the son in whom she had placed all her hopes for the future was now unemployed. Bruno had suffered a stroke some time before which left him partially paralysed so his wife had taken on more responsibility for teaching at the conservatory. Their daughter Maria had married, but the couple lived with them and Maria helped out with a certain amount of teaching. Heinz, having given up his studies at the Technical University in Dresden, had been obliged to accept work as a casual labourer, however he too was now unemployed. What was to become of them? One course of action was an appeal direct to the Reich President, Paul von Hindenburg. Heydrich had the support of his superiors at the Kiel naval base and sent a letter, through the correct channels, appealing against the decision.

In the meantime, the von Ostens heard of the dismissal and the reasons for it, they immediately forbid their daughter to have anything to do with the 'wayward young man', who was no longer considered a suitable match for their daughter. However, the von Ostens had not anticipated their daughter's tenacity and depth of love for Heydrich; refusing all parental advice, Lina remained true to her Reinhard, strengthening the bond of their relationship.

It was not long before the reply came from Berlin; the decision to terminate Heydrich from naval service was upheld and so with the die cast, Reinhard and Lina went to the local zoo in Halle to discuss alternatives for the future.

A position as instructor at the Hanseatic Yachting School in Neustadt become vacant with a salary of three hundred marks per month. In 1927, Heydrich had achieved a German Ostsee Master's certificate for the twelve foot dinghy and this was followed in 1928 with the equivalent for the North Sea. The Merchant Navy was also a consideration. Neither offered the miserable Heydrich the dreamed of military career with it's uniform and comradeship, for weeks he sulked at the few prospects now open to him. Heydrich found some consolation with his friend, Schultze, who was acquainted with Dr. Günther Gericke, a lawyer, local politician and member of the Reichstag for the Farmers' Party. He offered Heydrich a post with the Rural District Council, commanding a salary of three hundred and fifty marks per month, no small amount in those days; Heydrich was undecided and still yearned for a military position.

Freiherr von Eberstein, an old family friend of the Heydrichs

Elisabeth Heydrich had not always agreed with the intended marriage, considering Lina below their social standing. It was partly this concern over the family's social position that brought about the meeting between Reinhard Heydrich and Heinrich Himmler. Reinhard's godmother was a long-standing friend of the Heydrich family, and a member of the local aristocratic family, the von Ebersteins. Her son, Karl, was a senior member of the National Socialist 'Sturmabteilung', (SA), in Munich. Karl von Eberstein had direct contact with Captain Ernst Röhm, the SA Chief of Staff and, more importantly for Heydrich, the Reichsführer-SS, Heinrich Himmler. Elisabeth Heydrich enquired of her friend if 'Karlchen' might be in a position to recommend her son for a position within one of the military wings of the Party. This was, to her, socially acceptable; even the Baron von Eberstein was a member. Reinhard Heydrich was not interested in the SA as he considered this organisation scant compensation for the loss of his naval career. The 'Schutzstaffel' (Protection Group), or SS, however, posed a different question. Still in its infancy and little known outside the immediate political circles, the SS offered a more elite impression with its smart black uniform and strict discipline. Tentative enquiries were made with the result that Karl von Eberstein agreed to help.

It was only now that Heydrich agreed to join the NSDAP, probably to assist his application for the new job. His membership number was 544916 [1]. Heydrich travelled to Hamburg where, on 1st June 1931, he signed his application form to join the SS [2]. The completed paperwork, with a suitable portrait photograph attached, was passed, with recommendations from von Eberstein, through Röhm and finally came to rest on the desk of the Reichsführer-SS.

Himmler was impressed by the Nordic appearance of his latest applicant and even more so by his qualifications as a 'Nachrichtenoffizier' (Radio Officer) from the Navy. By coincidence, Hitler had just commissioned Himmler to provide an intelligence service for the SS, similar to that already in operation for the SA. He consulted with von Eberstein and agreed to see the 'Nachrichtenmann' in person. It appears that there is some substance in the claim that Himmler was confused with the distinction between a 'Nachrichtenoffizier' (Radio Officer) and a 'Nachrichtendienst-Offizier' (Intelligence Officer) as he had little military experience and none in the world of espionage. The date, 16th June 1931 was agreed, and then transmitted to Heydrich in Hamburg, for him to travel to Munich for a personal interview with Himmler [3].

Reichsführer-SS Himmler

Heydrich was preparing to leave on the fifteenth, when a telegram arrived from von Eberstein stating that Himmler was ill and unable to pursue the interview. In truth, another candidate had appeared on the scene and Himmler did not wish to make a quick decision. Heydrich was prepared to await the new appointment date, but Lina had other ideas; she ignored the cancellation and insisted that her fiancé travel to Munich as originally planned, sending von Eberstein a telegraph to the effect that Heydrich would arrive the following day. Taking the night train from Hamburg, he arrived in Munich early the following morning, much to the annoyance of von Eberstein who greeted him. Still unwilling to take his friend to see the Reichsführer, von Eberstein agreed to telephone Himmler at his home in the suburb of Waldtrudering. This placed Himmler on the spot, but he finally agreed to the visit.

Himmler at once explained his requirement to find an intelligence officer to organise a new Intelligence Service for the SS. Heydrich realised immediately that he did not have the appropriate qualifications, but decided to remain silent. Himmler asked his visitor to sketch out a plan for the new service and gave him twenty minutes for the task. An avid reader of numerous spy stories about the British Secret Service and with the little intelligence material he had encountered during his service days, Heydrich started to put together a plan with suitable military phrases, supported by a quickly drawn diagram to illustrate his ideas. The Reichsführer was impressed with the results, (his knowledge of the workings of an intelligence service was obviously less than that of Heydrich) and immediately agreed to employ the new man on his staff in Munich, beginning that August, at a salary of one hundred and eighty marks per month. The other applicant, a police captain named Horninger, was dropped at once and later proved to be a spy for the Munich police, whose task was to obtain inside information about the SS (a few years later, Horninger committed suicide [4]).

Heydrich returned north with the good news of his new position and on 14th July 1931 entered the Hamburg SS. The new recruit was given SS number 10120 [5] and the rank of SS-Mann. During the first weeks Heydrich experienced street fighting in the Dovenhof district at first hand, by 10th August 1931, he was officially transferred to Munich with the higher rank of SS-Sturmführer and placed on the staff of the 'Reichsführung-SS Oberstab', in charge of 'Abteilung Ic' [6].

As a result of his former career problems, the hoped for wedding date in September of 1931 did not materialise, but on 26th December 1931, (Herr von Osten's birthday), in the village church at Grossenbrode, Reinhard Heydrich and Lina von Osten became man and wife. Uniforms of the NSDAP had been banned just before, but this did not prevent the local SA and SS attending in white shirts, black trousers and riding boots. Reinhard Heydrich was uncomfortably dressed in top hat and morning suit', an entertaining sight for his new bride who described him as *"...looking like the manager of an amusement establishment! "*. The church, decorated above the altar with a swastika made of fir, was packed. The couple took their chosen vows, 'A solid castle is our God'. Reinhard's sister sang the 'Ave Maria' with a light soprano voice and Bruno ended the ceremony with his own composition. He sang 'Our Father'. As the couple walked down the aisle to leave, they passed under the raised arms of the SA and SS giving the Party salute and the 'Horst Wessel Lied' was played on the organ [7].

The Church was unhappy about the 'National Socialist' arrangements and the minister who conducted the service was moved shortly afterwards as a punishment for allowing the local SA and SS to attend [8]. Many years later, Lina was proud to relate that their wedding was still remembered by the locals as a happy occasion. At the reception that followed, street bunting was displayed and all the relations, got to know each other, in particular, the respective mothers-in-law got on very well [9]. Soon afterwards, the newly married couple travelled to Munich where they were to set up home.

JULFEST PRE-NUPTIALS

1.

2.

3.

4.

5.

THE ORIGINAL PHOTOGRAPH CAPTIONS HAVE BEEN USED FROM THIS HEYDRICH FAMILY ALBUM.

1. *"THE GABLE WINDOWS BELONG TO LINA'S ROOM".* 25.12.1931.

2. *"THE WEDDING CAKE - PLEASE TRY"* (the two mothers - left Frau von Osten and right Frau Heydrich). 25.12.1931

3. *"BROTHER & SISTER-IN-LAW WHILST CHOOSING THE SURPRISES FOR THE POLTERABEND".* 25.12.1931 (This refers to the custom of smashing china before the wedding).

4. *"MOTHER* (HEYDRICH) *WITH OUR TWO FATHERS"* 25.12.1931 (Left von Osten, centre Frau Elizabeth Heydrich and right Bruno Heydrich).

5. *"SO FINALLY THEY KEEP STILL"* 25.12.1931 (Lina and Reinhard at the von Osten family home).

THE WEDDING DAY

6.

7.

8.

9.

THE ORIGINAL PHOTOGRAPH CAPTIONS HAVE BEEN USED FROM THE HEYDRICH FAMILY ALBUM

6. *THE CHURCH AT GROSSENBRODE WHERE LINA AND HEYDRICH GOT MARRIED* 26.12.1931 (the photograph was taken in 1997).

7. *"SA WISHES 'HEIL' TO IT",* 26.12.1931 (Outside the Grossenbrode Church SS & SA men line the path awaiting Lina and Reinhard, it is interesting to note the plain white shirts and black ties as NSDAP uniforms had been banned at this time).

8. *"MRS. REINHARD HEYDRICH SAFELY LED ON THE WAY TO HAPPINESS".* 26.12.1931(Reinhard Heydrich in top hat !)

9. *"UP TO THE STRUGGLE"* 26.12.1931 (In other words, the struggle of life).

10.

11.

12.

10. *"THE YOUNG COUPLE AND HIS PARENTS"* 26.12.1931 (Left Bruno Heydrich, Lina and Reinhard, Frau Elizabeth Heydrich to the right).

11. *"THE YOUNG COUPLE AND HER PARENTS"* 26.12.1931 (Left Herr von Osten, Lina and Reinhard, Frau von Osten to the right).

12. *"....AND THEN...THREE CHEERS !"* 26.12.1931 (Lina and her new husband, her father Herr von Osten can be seen to the left).

CHAPTER 4
THE INFANT SECURITY SERVICE

Reinhard Heydrich had moved to Munich at the beginning of August 1931, before his transfer took effect and found lodgings with the widow, Frau Viktoria Edrich, on the fourth floor of Turkenstrasse 23 [1]. Frau Edrich was well known among the 'old fighters' of the NSDAP, and the sacred 'Blood Flag' is reputed to have been hidden at her apartment during the period of the ban on the SA and SS. On 11th August 1931, Heydrich wrote to his future in-laws, referring to them as his parents, "*I have now been here for ten days. I have settled into my work and have formed a picture of the range of work and the living possibilities. Yesterday, I received the decree of the Reichsführer with the directions of my department and was immediately promoted to Sturmführer with pay from 1st September........I have rented a very cheap, simple room in a nice area from a decent old lady....*" [2].

The 'Brown House', the new NSDAP headquarters where Heydrich had his first office

Richard Hildebrandt, Heydrich shared his first office with Hildebrandt

His office was set up in a room at the Brown House in Briennerstrasse, the new NSDAP headquarters, renovated from the original Barlow Palace. He was given a kitchen table and chair for furniture and shared the room with SS-Sturmbannführer Richard Hildebrandt, the Chief of Staff of "Sepp" Dietrich's SS-Group South. Heydrich was seven years younger than Hildebrandt, both men had travelled abroad extensively and it wasn't long before the two became friends.

Himmler had previously worked for Gregor Strasser and had begun to build up files from newspaper cuttings of the friends and enemies of the movement. Heydrich was handed these files and told to organise them into a chronological filing system. To his disappointment, his chief had retained the nominal title of Director of the Ic Service, but he certainly kept none of it's duties. The term 'Ic' was derived from the German General Staff's meaning of 'enemy reconnaissance'. It was Heydrich's job to discover news articles and other interesting items and then paste them into files. He did not even have his own typewriter and borrow ed Hildebrandt's on an hourly basis. Unassisted, he organised this basic filing system, using newspaper cuttings, brush, paste and index cards contained in cigar boxes. This then was the birth of the Sicherheitsdienst, or SD.

Heydrich endevoured to identify and catalogue the enemies of the NSDAP, these were sectioned under headings such as Communists, Socialists, the German Nationalist Party, the Catholic Centre Party and the German People's Party. Also seen as working against the movement and therefore worthy of attention, were Freemasons, Marxists, the political Church and Jews (at this stage, Jews were seen as political enemies and not a racial threat). It is important to note that Heydrich did not have exclusivity for security within the NSDAP, at this stage others were also building security or intelligence services.

At about the same time as Heydrich's arrival in the SS, the 'Gaupropagandaleiter' for Munich and Upper Bavaria, Rauscher, had started to build an intelligence organisation for the Party in the Brown House. Politically striving for the same goals, Rauscher and Heydrich nevertheless became staunch rivals. Rauscher's service was soon shown to be somewhat inept in it's handling of sensitive information at the district level. Several reports appeared in local newspapers entitled 'intimate revelations from the Brown House', Rauscher's service was soon discovered as the source and thereafter faded from view.

The SA also had it's own intelligence service with Dr. Graf Karl DuMoulin-Eckart as it's chief. If one considers that the SS was still, in these early years, part of, and subordinate to, the much larger and important SA, it becomes obvious that Heydrich's position was precarious. Himmler was still junior to Ernst Röhm and, consequently, any attempts to usurp the power of the SA had to be handled delicately. The SA Intelligence Service had sufficient personnel and financing. It was only when the SA Intelligence Chief and spy Du Moulin-Eckart was publicly exposed as a spy by the Social-Democrat newspaper 'Münchener Post' that his organisation began to weaken and the infant SS Intelligence Service grew considerably in stature. Can one suspect intrigue in these events or was it just good fortune for Heydrich? Admittedly, Heydrich's name also appeared in the article as 'Leutnant Heyderich', but nothing was mentioned further about his duties and he remained a dark figure in the background to all but those in high office at the 'Brown House'.

Soon after, in November 1931, Heydrich uncovered a Munich Putsch veteran as a member of the Bavarian Political Police who had been passing on information to his authorities about the NSDAP. Instead of exposing him, Heydrich managed to change his allegiance to the SS Intelligence Service. From that day on regular reports from within the Bavarian Political Police Office landed on Heydrich's desk, with information in the opposite direction drying up completely.

SS-Sturmführer Reinhard Heydrich had certainly made an impression. The Reichsführer rewarded him with a promotion on 1st December 1931 to SS-Hauptsturmführer [3] and effectively this gave Heydrich a rank higher than that with which he left the Navy only eight months previously. Himmler had recognised the growing importance of his intelligence service and agreed to a relocation of it's office. This was not only as it had increased it's volume of work, but also to afford a means of protection away from the prying eyes in the Brown House. Heydrich was also allowed three assistants. The most suitable location was considered to be Heydrich's lodgings at Turkenstrasse 23 and an extra room was obtained for the purpose. So this was the first independent office of the SD [4]. The same desk and chair were moved to the new rooms, but the office still lacked a typewriter, Hildebrandt's continued to be borrowed, but this time it had to be carried across from Briennerstrasse.

As a wedding present to his protégé, Himmler promoted Heydrich to SS-Sturmbannführer on 25th December 1931 [5]. The newly-weds arrived in Munich soon after and temporarily occupied one of the rooms at the SD Office. Heydrich found an apartment for his new bride at Lochhausen, in house number 55. They busied themselves with decorating and Lina soon became friends with a Bavarian woman living in one of the other appartments, who taught Lina Bavarian customs and cooking.

The Heydrichs received an invitation to visit the Reichsführer at his home in Waldtrudering and they travelled across town with Hildebrandt. They were greeted by Himmler and his wife Marge. Also present was another woman, Edith von Coler, a cousin of Frau Himmler. Hildebrandt remained quiet, his wife left at home, having just given birth to a child. That afternoon, Lina accompanied the men on a stroll through the village and Himmler enquired of her background. Later, at coffee, the discussion turned to race and origins. Lina realised that this was not just a social get-together and became upset on the way home. She would never feel comfortable about this type of discussion [6].

In February 1932, Heydrich was shocked to hear of the arrest of one of his men in Oldenburg. The agent admitted under interrogation that he had passed on information to Hans Kobelinski, the Ic man for the Braunschweig SS sub-district. Luckily, the police never discovered his true identity, but the affair had given Heydrich a fright. Not wishing to suffer the same fate as DuMoulin, Heydrich realised he would have to reorganise his intelligence service and it's system of recruitment. In future, all applicants would have to be screened by SD Central Office and have the personal authorisation of Heydrich.

This moved Heydrich to consider his use of assistants and the desire for them to be independent of the Party, in fact of the SS itself. He removed all SD informers and counter-espionage agents from the SS and made them personally accountable to himself. Heydrich's SD was to be a separate entity within the SS, but maintaining an amount of independence from the main body of the SS. The SS has often been described as a 'State within the National Socialist State' and this was how Heydrich now viewed his SD within the SS.

In April 1932, the SS and SA were both declared prohibited organisations by the Weimar Government. This move sounded the death toll for the remains of DuMoulin's SA Intelligence Service, which did not re-appear when the ban was lifted in the autumn of the same year. Thereafter, for the duration of the prohibition, the SD was to be known as the Press and Information Service (PID).

Later that same month, with the intention of recruiting more assistants, Heydrich set out on a grand tour of Germany to visit his provincial offices. He had decided to run his SD along the lines of the British Secret Service, which he greatly admired. He even liked to be known as 'C', the term used for the head of the British Secret Service [7]. His recruitment drive produced some interesting results from the ranks of German academics. One of the first successes was Paul Leffler, an industrialist and qualified hydraulics engineer. The lawyer and political economist, Dr. Herbert Mehlhorn, was another drawn into the net, and who later rose to the SS rank of Oberführer [8]. They were followed by Dr. Wilhelm Albert and Dr. Johannes Schmidt. Final mention must be made here of Carl-Albrecht Oberg, a merchant from Hamburg, who was destined to become the Higher SS and Police Leader in France with the rank of SS-Obergruppenführer [9]. Heydrich not only screened these men himself, but also had dossiers on their wives.

During these last months before the legal seizure of power by Hitler, Heydrich secretly recruited and built up his security service from among the intellectuals in Germany. Himmler was so impressed that on 19th July 1932, he officially recognised the title of 'Sicherheitsdienst' (Security Service) or 'SD' as the organisation was more generally known. and named Heydrich as it's Director [10]. On 29th July, he promoted his zealous chief of security to the rank of SS-Standartenführer [11]. A move to larger premises for the SD was indicated.

At the end of September 1932, the Heydrichs moved from their apartment in Lochhausen and the SD entourage also moved from Turkenstrasse, both occupying a small villa next to the grounds of Schloss Nymphenburg, at Zuccalistrasse 4 [12]. The rent was 180 marks. The Heydrichs occupied a small flat, whilst the remainder of the building was used by seven assistants as the SD Central Office. The house was surrounded by a garden and fencing at the end of a cul-de-sac. Lina prepared the food for all and looked after the whole house.

New equipment and furniture were bought with the little amount of money available, but ongoing payment of additional wages were a problem and Heydrich without success continuously bombarded Himmler with his department's financial problems and requests for extra cash. Even the telephone was disconnected on one occasion through failure to pay the bill. Eventually, Ernst Röhm agreed to visit the SD Central Office with Rudolf Hess, and Heydrich stressed to everyone how important this visit could prove to be in achieving extra funding.

In the meantime, the daily routine of running the office continued. In the hall were two great coke burning stoves, providing heating for the house. It was the duty of the SD's factotum, i.e. Frau Lina Heydrich, to light these stoves every morning, she stored the matches above one of the stoves. Every day, these matches had disappeared, resulting in Lina having to buy extra. The twenty-one year old housewife finally lost her patience and bought a box of joke exploding matches from the market in Munich, replacing the genuine ones on the shelf above the stove.

That same morning, Heydrich received a call from Himmler saying that the promised visit would take place that very day and, in fact, Röhm and Hess were already on their way. A quick tidying up ensued and Lina was ushered out to buy cigars for the exalted guests. It wasn't long before their car arrived and they were beginning their inspection. SD assistants were introduced to the men, followed by an explanation of the workings of the office. Lina patiently waited downstairs and provided the cigars and some port at the conclusion of the inspection tour. Secretary Josef Strohmeier took out his matches to offer a light for Röhm's cigar, when suddenly there was an almighty "bang"! Röhm turned white and Himmler looked for cover. These were turbulent times indeed. Lina quickly put their minds at rest with an explanation and all found the event amusing. The match thief had been uncovered and Röhm promised a new injection of cash. Heydrich's worries were relaxed.

Above left: The SD 'Headquarters' at Turkenstrasse 23, (photograph taken in 1997).
Above right: Both the Heydrichs and the SD moved into the pleasant villa, Zuccalistrasse 4, next to the grounds of Schloss Nymphenburg.

Dr.Graf Karl Du Moulin-Eckart the SA's Intelligence Chief standing with SA-Stabschef Röhm.

Heydrich managed to recruit some excellent German academics into his Security Service, including, from left, Carl-Albrecht Oberg, Dr.Wilhelm Albert, Dr.Johannes Schmidt and Dr.Herbert Mehlhorn.

CHAPTER 5
QUESTIONABLE BLOOD

Heydrich's fortunes had certainly improved. The desired career in uniform had finally materialised and his position in the local leadership of the Party looked set to rise. He had found a position that suited his talents. If the Navy did not desire his services, then what better than a career in another of his boyhood loves; the world of intrigue and espionage.

Gauleiter Rudolf Jordan

Rudolf Jordan was the Gauleiter for the district of Halle-Merseburg, which included Heydrich's birthplace and family home. On 6th June 1932, he signed a letter addressed to Gregor Strasser, one of the important Party (NSDAP) leaders in Munich. Two days later, the letter arrived on Strasser's desk causing immediate consternation in the halls of National Socialist power.

Jordan wrote, *"It has come to my attention that there is, in the Reich leadership organisation, a party member with the name Heydrich, whose father lives in Halle. There is reason to believe that the Bruno Heydrich indicated as his father is a Jew. I enclose an excerpt from Hugo Riemanns Musik Lexikon of 1916, published by Max Hesses, Berlin W15.......as proof."* This excerpt noted that Bruno Heydrich's name was really 'Süss', a well known Jewish name [1].

Strasser recognised at once the importance of this information. Until now he had little or no contact with the young SS security man, Reinhard Heydrich, but the news from Halle had serious implications. There was now the suggestion that Heydrich could be an impostor who had infiltrated the innermost sanctum of the Party. He had gained the confidence of not only the Reichsführer SS, but of Hitler himself. Wheels were immediately set in motion to discover the truth. Dr. Achim Gercke, the Party's expert on race, was tasked with the job of investigating Heydrich's background.

On 22nd June 1932 Dr. Gercke reported, that *".......Oberleutnant of Sea, Reinhardt (sic) Heydrich, is of German origin and free from any coloured and Jewish blood".* He went on to explain the misunderstanding over the name 'Süss' [2].

The confusion had arisen when Heydrich's paternal grandmother, Ernestine Wilhelmine Heydrich, born Lindner, had lost her husband and married for the second time. Her new husband was a locksmith by the name of Gustav Robert Süss and, as she had a large family by her first husband, Reinhard Heydrich, she often called herself Süss-Heydrich. This was obviously to avoid any confusion. Gercke maintained that,*'Süss' was, in any case......not of Jewish origin."* He was an Evangelist. The fact that Reinhard had no direct line of descent from the locksmith, provided conclusive proof. The chief of the SD was pure Aryan.

The findings of the investigation were passed to all interested parties, however, the stigma of Jewish blood remained with Heydrich throughout his life and even continued after his death. Rumours were still rife in Halle, where, in December 1940, the then SS-Gruppenführer had to resort to legal action against a local baker by the name of Johannes Pabst who had been spreading gossip [3]. Pabst, a local NSDAP member, received twelve months imprisonment on 12th December and the local press trumpeted *"A Year's Imprisonment For The Slanderer!"* Heydrich always believed that the rumours were seized upon by his enemies in the Party who encouraged them and gleaned a great deal of enjoyment from the distress that they caused.

Even after the war the rumours persisted. The SD officer, SS-Sturmbannführer Dr.Wilhelm Höttl, who gave evidence at Nuremburg, stated in his memoirs that Heydrich had arranged to have all the Halle administrative records edited to erase all question of his Jewish origins [4]. The records of his birth were supposedly stolen. Apparently, he also had a gravestone in the cemetery at Meissen, near Leipzig, removed because it bore the name of his grandmother, Sarah Heydrich. The replacement read 'S. Heydrich'. In 1945, Dr. Wilhelm Stuckart, the Secretary of State in the Interior Ministry and a SS-Obergruppenführer in the Reich Security Service, stated that he was sure that Heydrich was Jewish or partly Jewish [5]. Another source, Helmut Maurer, of the Counter-Intelligence Service, insisted that he had taken incriminating evidence from the

Halle records office and handed it to Admiral Wilhelm Canaris for future use against the SD chief [6]. The fact is, Heydrich's birth is clearly recorded in the birth register in Halle under number 669, dated 12th March 1904 [7]. Even so, the local authorities stressed that this is 'believed to be the entry of birth for Reinhard Heydrich' [8]. It is incredible how far a rumour can spread, even to the point of some individuals making mention of Heydrich's 'hooked nose', the shape of which was due in part to it having been broken twice, once in a pentathlon competition and once whilst on a private ride. The contents of Canaris' safe were discovered at Zossen in Spring 1945 and although they contained much material on the anti-Hitler circle, there was no mention of Heydrich's ancestry.

Mention must be made here of two other versions of Heydrich's so-called Jewish origins. The first being the Swedish masseur and confidant of Himmler, Felix Kersten. He insists in his memoirs (which should be viewed with caution), that not only Himmler, but Hitler also knew of Heydrich's Jewish ancestry from the early years. According to Kersten, Hitler had conducted a private interview with his security chief on this very subject and had determined to retain his services, reporting to Himmler, *"This Heydrich is a highly talented, but also highly dangerous man whose abilities we must retain in the movement.......He will be eternally grateful to us for retaining him rather than throwing him out and will obey us blindly "* [9]. Himmler had also, apparently, acted as a sort of mentor to his protégé, in order to help him overcome his inner torment. Himmler's efforts were successful, Kersten continues, *"...for Heydrich had soon conquered the Jew in him on a purely intellectual level and had taken up an extreme position on the other side"* [10]. The British historian, Hugh Trevor-Roper, respected in some circles, was convinced by Kersten's version of events, even though many parts of Kersten's memoirs have been shown to be somewhat suspect. Writing the foreword to Kersten's work, he declared, *"...with all the authority that I possess, for despite his blond hair and blue eyes he was, as Himmler and Hitler were fully aware, of Jewish origin."* In 1962, he wrote incredibly, *"Fear of blackmail was behind Heydrich's success"* [11].

Are we to believe that Hitler would have been prepared to risk everything in those early days in order to retain the services of a man he considered dangerous. Heydrich was only dangerous because of his position and a simple termination of his employment would have been sufficient to sever any threat to the Party. In 1935, Himmler certainly had no qualms about sacking his ultra efficient head of the 'SS Hauptamt' (SS Head Office), SS-Gruppenführer Kurt Wittje, when it came to light that he was a practising homosexual [12].

An even more ridiculous version was put forward by the British writer, Charles Wighton. He suggests that Gercke, having found no evidence in the allegation of Jewish blood on Heydrich's paternal lineage, discovered Jewish ancestry on his mother's side. In evidence, he states that Gercke investigated Heydrich's mother, but went no further. He concludes that the maternal grandmother, named Mautsch, was of Jewish descent and that Lina Heydrich had admitted that *"she was the one who brought the money into the family"* [13]. Wighton also states that Gercke's investigations took a year and the results were produced in 1933, after the National Socialist seizure of power, clearly intimating a 'doctored' report. Anyone can see the date on Gercke's findings is 22nd June 1932 [14], fourteen days after the receipt of Jordan's letter and over seven months before the National Socialists came to power.

Heydrichs' grandmother
Ernestine Heydrich

Heydrich, his blood was
found to be pure

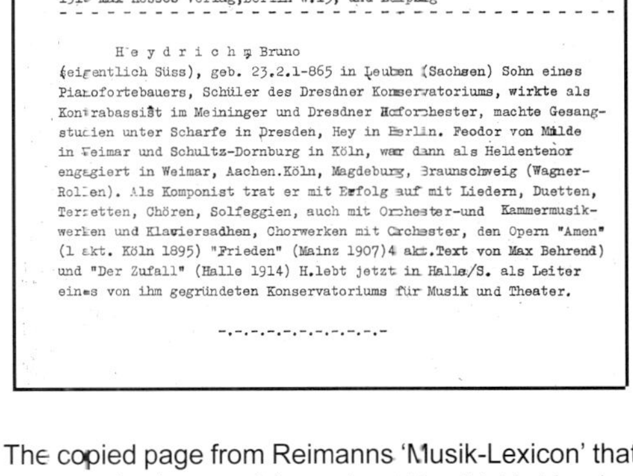

Aus dem Buch
Hugo Riemanns Musik-Lexikon
1916 Max Hesses Verlag, Berlin W.15, und Leipzig

- -

H e y d r i c h, Bruno
(eigentlich Süss), geb. 23.2.1-865 in Leuben (Sachsen) Sohn eines Pianofortebauers, Schüler des Dresdner Konservatoriums, wirkte als Kontrabassist im Meininger und Dresdner Hoforchester, machte Gesangstudien unter Scharfe in Dresden, Hey in Berlin. Feodor von Milde in Weimar und Schultz-Dornburg in Köln, war dann als Heldentenor engagiert in Weimar, Aachen.Köln, Magdeburg, Braunschweig (Wagner-Rollen). Als Komponist trat er mit Erfolg auf mit Liedern, Duetten, Terzetten, Chören, Solfeggien, auch mit Orchester-und Kammermusikwerken und Klaviersachen, Chorwerken mit Orchester, den Opern "Amen" (1 akt. Köln 1895) "Frieden" (Mainz 1907)4 akt.Text von Max Behrend) und "Der Zufall" (Halle 1914) H.lebt jetzt in Halle/S. als Leiter eines von ihm gegründeten Konservatoriums für Musik und Theater.

-.-.-.-.-.-.-.-.-.-

The copied page from Reimanns 'Musik-Lexicon' that made Jordan suspicious about Heydrich's blood

Nationalsozialistische Deutsche Arbeiterpartei
Gauleitung Halle-Merseburg

Halle a. S. 2, Postschließfach 335
Fernspr.-Sammelnummer 27111

Postscheck: K. Richter, Halle
Amt Leipzig Nr. 29716

Abt.: Jo/Br.
Streng Vertraulich!

Halle (Saale), den 6. Juni 1932
Thielenstr. 5

8. Juni 1932

Herrn
Gregor Strasser,
München

Lieber Pg. Strasser!

Wie mir zu Ohren gekommen ist, befindet sich in der Reichsleitung ein Pg. mit dem Namen Heydrich, dessen Vater in Halle wohnen soll. Es besteht Veranlassung zu vermuten, dass der als Vater bezeichnete Bruno Heydrich in Halle Jude ist. Jch gebe Jhnen in der Anlage einen Auszug aus Hugo Riemanns-Musik Lexikon 1916 Max Hesses Verlag Berlin W.15, aus welchem Sie alles Nähere ersehen können. Vielleicht wäre es angebracht, dass die Personalabteilung einmal diese Sache prüfen könnte.

Mit Hitler Heil!

Jhr sehr ergebener

Gauleiter

1 Anlage!

Above left: The original letter sent on 6th June 1932 by Gauleiter Jordan, questioning Heydrichs' blood.
Above right:Dr.Archim Gercke, the 'race' expert'. He was asked to fully investigate Heydrich's racial lineage.

N.S. Auskunft

(Briefanschrift: Reichsleitung der N.S.D.A.P. (N.S Auskunft) München 43, Postfach 80)

München, den 22. Juni 1932

Unser Zeichen: U 31 Dr. G/E.
Ihr Zeichen:

Betrifft:

Gutachten

über die rassische Herkunft des Oberleutnant z.See a.D.

Reinhardt Heydrich.

Aus beiliegender Ahnenliste geht hervor, dass Oberleutnant z.See a. D. Reinhardt Heydrich deutscher Herkunft ist und frei von farbigem und jüdischem Blutseinschlag.

Das für die Familie Heydrich beleidigende Gerücht, dass sie ehem Süss geheissen habe, das dazu geführt hat, den Vater von Oberleut. Heydrich im Volksmunde als " Isidor Süss" zu bezeichnen und das schliesslich zu der Vermutung Anlass gegeben hat, dass die Familie jüdischer Herkunft sei, hat folgenden Hintergrund. Aus der Ahnenliste ist ersichtlich dass Oberleutnant Heydrichs Grossmutter Ernestine Wilhelmine Heydrich. geborene Lindner (in der Ahnenliste unter Nr 5) in zweiter Ehe mit dem Schlossergehilfen Gustav Robert Süss verheiratet war und als Mutter einer zahlreichen Kinderschar aus der ers Ehe mit ihrem ersten Mann Reinhold Heydrich sich des öfteren Süss - Heydrich genannt hat. Es ist übrigens hierbei bemerkenswert, dass auch der Schlossergehilfe Süss nicht jüdischer Herkunft ist. Diese zweite Ehe der Mutter von Bruno Heydrich führte zu der falschen Annahme, die in "Riemanns Musiker- Lexikon" von 1916 durch die Bemerkung "Heydrich (eigentlich Süss)" Verbreitung fand. In späteren Auflagen dieses Lexikons wurde dieser falsche Zusatz unterlassen und zwar auf Veranlassung der Familie Heydrich.

Zusammenfassend stelle ich danach fest, dass der Vorwurf, dass die Familie Heydrich jüdischer Herkunft sei oder früher einen anderen Namen führte, unrichtig ist.

Für die Richtigkeit dieses Gutachtens übernehme ich die volle Verantwortung und erkläre mich bereit, es notfalls auch vor Gericht zu vertreten.

Behauptungen, die dieses Gutachten zu entkräften suchen, können nur auf Grund einer das Gegenteil aussagenden Urkunde gemacht werden. Sämtliche Angaben beruhen auf urkundlichen Belegen, die auf ihre Stichhaltigkeit hin geprüft worden sind.

Heil!

Dr. Gercke

Above: Document dated 22nd June 1932, from Dr.Gercke stating that Heydrich is totally free from any Jewish blood and outlines how the question had arisen. A copy of this letter was sent to Gauleiter Jordan and to the other main offices including the Reichsleitung der SS.

Wilhelm Höttl

One of Heydrich's SD officers. Höttl's post war testimony encouraged the myth that Heydrich had Jewish ancestry.

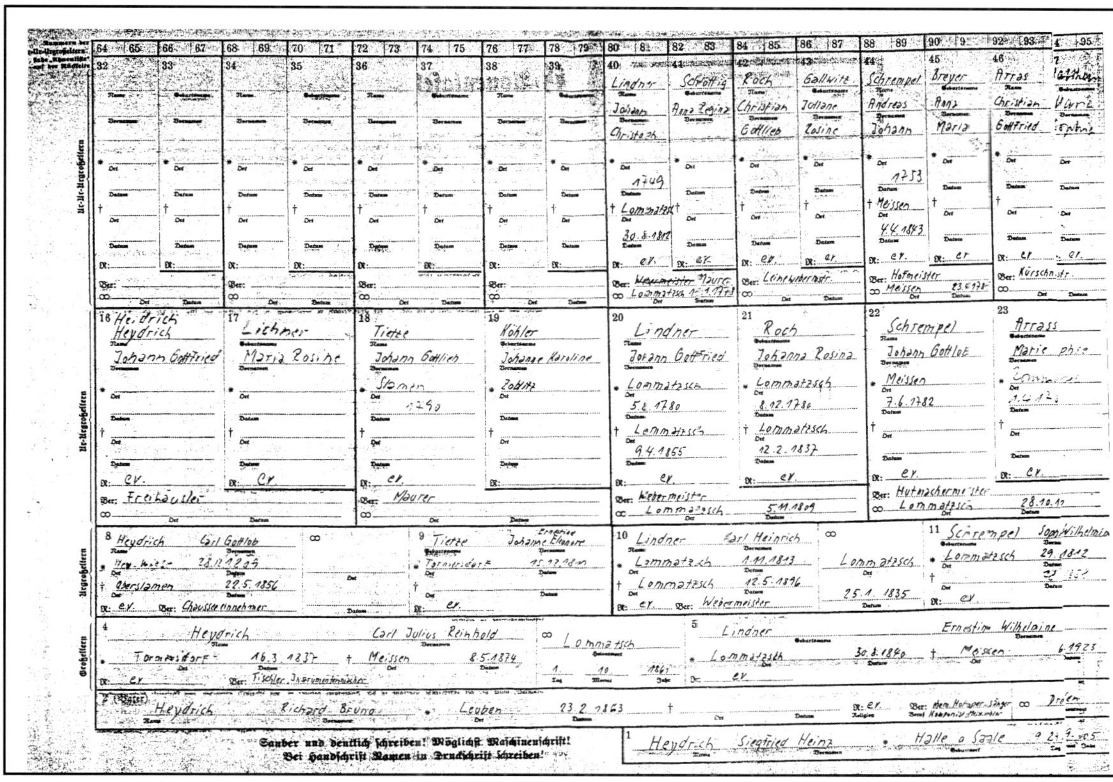

1 Heydrich, Siegfried Heinz, * Halle a. Saale

2 (Vater) Heydrich, Richard Bruno, * Leuben 23.2.1863

4 Heydrich, Carl Julius Reinhold, * Tornesdorf 16.3.1837, † Meissen 8.5.1874

5 Lindner, Ernestine Wilhelmine, * Lommatzsch 30.2.1840, † Meissen 6.1923

8 Heydrich, Carl Gottlob, † Oberslamen 22.5.1856, Ber.: Chausseeeinnehmer

9 Tietze, Johanne Ernestine Eleonore, * Tornesdorf

10 Lindner, Carl Heinrich, * Lommatzsch 1.11.1813, † Lommatzsch 12.5.1896, Ber.: Webermeister

11 Schrempel, Sophie Wilhelmine, * Lommatzsch

16 Heydrich, Johann Gottfried, Ber.: Freihäusler

17 Löhmer, Maria Rosine

18 Tietze, Johann Gottlieb, Ber.: Maurer

19 Köhler, Johanne Karoline

20 Lindner, Johann Gottfried, * Lommatzsch 5.2.1780, † Lommatzsch 9.4.1855, Ber.: Webermeister

21 Roch, Johanna Rosina, * Lommatzsch 8.12.1786, † Lommatzsch 12.2.1837

22 Schrempel, Johann Gottlob, * Meissen 7.6.1782, Ber.: Hutmachermeister

23 Arrass, Marie Sophie

Sauber und deutlich schreiben! Möglichst Maschinenschrift! Bei Handschrift Namen in Druckschrift schreiben!

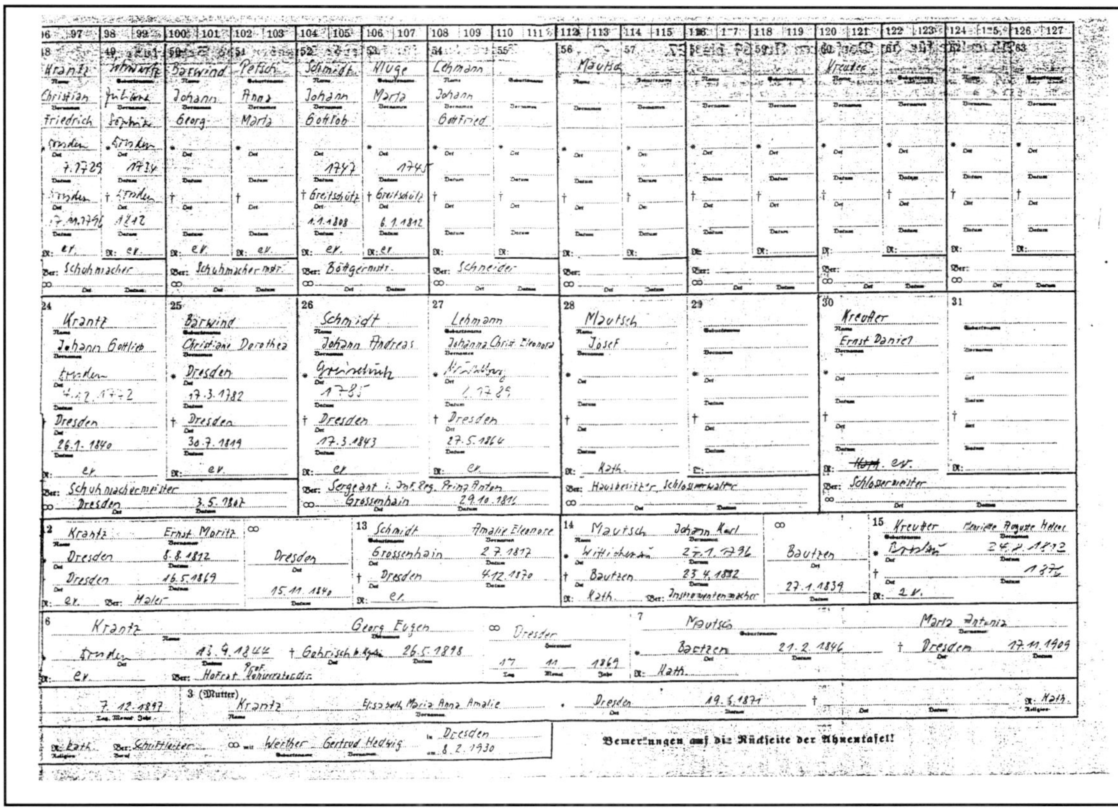

3 (Mutter) Krantz, Elisabeth Maria Anna Amalie, * Dresden 19.6.1871

6 Krantz, Georg Eugen, * 13.9.1844, † Gohrisch 26.5.1898, Ber.: Hofrat, Konservatoriumsdir.

7 Mautsch, Maria Antonia, * Bautzen 21.2.1846, † Dresden 17.11.1909

12 Krantz, Ernst Moritz, * Dresden 6.8.1812, † Dresden 16.5.1869, Ber.: Maler

13 Schmidt, Amalie Eleonore, * Grossenhain 2.7.1817, † Dresden 4.12.1870

14 Mautsch, Johann Karl, * 27.1.1796, † Bautzen 23.4.1882, Ber.: Instrumentenmacher

15 Kreuter, Henriette Auguste Helene

24 Krantz, Johann Gottlieb, † Dresden 26.1.1840, Ber.: Schuhmachermeister

25 Barwind, Christiane Dorothea, * Dresden 17.3.1782, † Dresden 30.7.1819

26 Schmidt, Johann Andreas, † Dresden 17.3.1843, Ber.: Sergeant i. Inf. Reg. Prinz Anton

27 Lehmann, Johanna Christ. Eleonore, † Dresden 27.5.1864

28 Mautsch, Josef, Ber.: Hausbesitzer, Schlosserwalter

30 Kreuter, Ernst Daniel, Ber.: Schlossermeister

Bemerkungen auf die Rückseite der Ahnentafel!

The official 'Ahnentafel' (document of family ancestry) for Reinhard Heydrich's brother Heinz

Unfortunately Reinhard Heydrich's offcial 'Ahnentafel' is no longer available from his SS file, having been stolen postwar, however the above example relating to his brother Heinz is still retained within his file. Where possible the ancestral line has been taken back to the 1700's. Sections not filled in relate to information that could not be found from church registers. It was common during the 1700's for church registers not to be scrupulously maintained and such omissions occur on many 'Ahnentafel'. However, those who wish to continue the question of Heydrich having Jewish blood will always use such omissions to fuel their argument.

CHAPTER 6
REINS OF POWER

For the young Reinhard Heydrich, the year 1933 began with worries over finance. Donations from the Party had ceased and his small department began to experience the gradual erosion of willing employees prepared to remain and continue working with little or no hope of payment. Lina prepared communal meals to save money. The SD menu often consisted of nothing more than vegetable soup or herring salad, (without the herring!) The outlook was bleak, but salvation was at hand.

The elections of 31st July 1932 saw the NSDAP gaining 13.8 million votes and 230 seats in the Reichstag [1]. It was now the largest single party in the seat of government. A further election on 6th November resulted in a reduction of 2 million votes [2], but nobody could deny that Hitler's party was a force to be reckoned with. The ageing President Hindenburg was reluctant to hand power to the 'Bohemian corporal', but after negotiations, he finally succumbed and, on 30th January 1933, declared Adolf Hitler, Reich Chancellor of Germany [3].

Hitler's new cabinet included the non-Nazi Franz von Papen as Vice-Chancellor, Konstantin von Neurath as Foreign Minister, Wilhelm Frick as Minister of the Interior, Werner von Blomberg as Defence Minister, Josef Goebbels as Minister for Enlightenment and Propaganda and the ever faithful Hermann Göring, already President of the Reichstag, as Minister President of Prussia [4]. Göring controlled the executive of two thirds of Germany, including the Prussian Police. Heinrich Himmler, along with his disciple, Heydrich, failed to obtain cabinet recognition and had to be content with the comparative minor role of Chief of the Bavarian Police [5]. Also left in the political wilderness was Ernst Röhm.

Three days before the seizure of power, Heydrich was ordered to relinquish his position as SD Chief and became attached to the personal staff of the Reichsführer-SS with 'special duties' [6]. This placed him at Himmler's side as one of the most important SS leaders.

On 27th February, at 9.14pm, a fire alarm was activated at Firehouse No. 6 on Linienstrasse in Berlin. The Reichstag building was in flames. The argument continues to this day over who was responsible. Heydrich has been suggested as the planner and many commissions and inquiries have delivered differing versions of the events. One thing we do know is that the fire gave Hitler the opportunity to request emergency powers from Hindenburg which in turn allowed him the authority required to implement many of his policies throughout the life of the Third Reich.

The government in Bavaria was reluctant to adhere to NSDAP rule, resulting in the National Socialist General Franz Ritter von Epp being submitted for appointment as State Commissioner. At a meeting between Himmler, Röhm, Gauleiter Adolf Wagner and Minister President Heinrich Held on 9th March, the Bavarian Ministry head refused to comply [7]. Epp's letter of authority had already been prepared in Berlin and was subsequently transmitted by telegram to the Bavarian authorities. All depended on the receipt of the telegram, which could easily have gone astray. Without this significant telegram, the National Socialists had no legal right to exercise executive power. Heydrich recognised the importance of this communication and went to the telegraph office in Munich, pistol in hand. The due process of law was complied with and the same night Epp formed a National Socialist Bavarian State Government. Wagner was appointed Minister of the Interior and Himmler became Chief of Police for the City of Munich. Heydrich was rewarded with the position of Director of Political Department VI and moved into the Police Headquarters with his boss [8].

Lina described the National Socialist seizure of power in Bavaria in a letter to her parents, dated 13th March 1933:

"Dear Parents,
What a life! You will surely have heard of our small revolution from the newspapers. From what Reinhard says, it must have been delightful. Well I will tell you how I experienced the affair. On Wednesday, Reinhard comes home early with the news, but he must return immediately to the Brown House, the Bavarian government does not wish to submit..........Around eleven o'clock Reinhard phones me. I should immediately send his pistol to the Brown House. Naturally, I immediately think the worst and am thoroughly shocked. At one o'clock the government gave instructions to the police to immediately shoot at the SA if they move against the government on the instructions of the Reich Chancellor. On hearing this, Röhm, Himmler and Reinhard drive to see Minister President Held and spend a whole hour negotiating with him. Röhm demands

that Epp should be voted in as Commissioner. They promise to do this by three o'clock...........The clock struck three, no answer. A telephone call from Röhm to Hitler results in the sending of a telegram. General Epp is installed as Commissioner by the Reich government, but for still unexplained reasons, the telegram does not arrive. A second is sent and Reinhard drives to the telegraph office and a half hour later has the memorable telegram in his hand. He delivers it to General Epp and suddenly things happen swiftly. First the occupation of the Police Headquarters. They drive there in four cars. In the first black SA vehicle are Epp and Röhm, in the second are Himmler and Reinhard. the other two are the escort. The guard is taken by surprise and act subdued. President Koch had already left the building. Reinhard says he gained much satisfaction from this, that the same person who half a year earlier had locked up the SA and the SS and had beat them with rubber truncheons, could not face those same people with a straight spine. Himmler becomes Chief of Police, Seidel-Dittmarsch Assistant-Chief and Reinhard, now don't laugh, Commissioner of the Political Police. I laughed so hard. When Reinhard's predecessor, senior government adviser Koch, was informed of this order, he went very pale. Reinhard, however, only wishes to 'muck out' there and then withdraw from the post. He could not bear the stench of so much manure in the long term, he says, it would suffocate..........Well, that was the police action. At the same time the other public buildings were occupied. Everything ran as planned without a shot being fired. The cleansing of the Munich Post was amusing. That is the newspaper of the Munich SPD. Standartenführer Höflich moved in with SA and SS people. The entire building was as if dead. They found about three hundred Reich opponents in a large salon. It conjures a pretty picture. All three hundred hold both hands in the air; politely commanded, hands down, left turn, march, march. In the evening especially the SA and SS had such fun. They were tasked to arrest all political opponents so far as they were known and take them to the Brown House..........Over two hundred are now in custody, KPD, SPD, Jews and Bavarian Peoples Party..........Höflich receives the order to arrest the Interior Minister Stutzel. Firstly the detainee says a quiet farewell to his wife and child, but then refuses to leave his bed and go with them. As he refuses the third request, they take him as he is and sit him in the car - and off to the Brown House. You can imagine the uproar. The Interior Minister stands in the hall in socks and nightshirt surrounded by loads of SA and SS people who don't know what to do for laughing. Then they approach him and stand on the crying minister's big toe with their heavy boots so he hops between them from one foot to the other. I'm sure you can picture it. As next the Jew Levy is led in. They make short shrift of him. They hit him with dog whips, take his shoes and socks off and so he must walk barefoot escorted by SS to his sparse cell. His house was in the meantime well fumigated. He was namely the leader of the Munich Jews. It paints a fine picture, that is how things are happening here. Many Jesuits and Jews fled from here. None are dead, none are mortally injured, but fear, fear I can tell you" [9].

Heydrich decided to open a Berlin office and suitable premises were found at Branitzerplatz, on the corner of Eichenallee. Lina also describes the move of the Munich SD office to Leopoldstrasse. Just off Leopoldstrasse is Ainmillerstrasse and it was here, at number 10, where Heydrich moved [10]. During these early months, Heydrich travelled daily to his police office, using the street car or his official car and not returning until late at night. He had little personal time left for his wife, whilst affairs of state kept him occupied. However when Lina contracted a chest infection and was kept in hospital for several days, her husband was by her side. On her discharge, he took her to Riederau on the Ammersee and there they stayed with the family Wulfert whilst she recovered.

Meanwhile, in February, Heydrich had been despatched to attend the second International Disarmament Conference in Geneva. Although not attending as part of the German delegation, Heydrich and his SS colleague, Friedrich-Wilhelm Krüger, were designated as police and security experts [11]. The twenty-eight year old inexperienced Heydrich was unfamiliar with the process of international negotiations and found the whole procedure rather difficult to handle. The head of the German delegation, Ambassador Rudolf Nadolny, a professional diplomat, was plainly embarrassed by the brash young man eager to influence his fellow delegates with National Socialist virtues. On several occasions, he had to be reminded that not all representatives were impressed by his political persuasion. The final show-down came when Heydrich complained to the manager of the German delegation's hotel that all the national flags of participating

Friedrich-Wilhelm Krüger

Ambassador Rudolf Nadolny

Auszug aus den Bestimmungen für Wochenkarten.

Die Wochenkarten sind streng persönlich und gelten nur für den Inhaber, dessen Lichtbild und Unterschrift sie tragen.

Wochenkarten, deren Kontrollnummer mit der Kontrollnummer des Wertscheines nicht übereinstimmt, sind ungültig.

Direktion der städt. Straßenbahnen.

Städtische Strassenbahnen München.

Wochenkarte

Name Heydrich Reinh.

Ainmillerstr. 10

ist bei Vorzeigung dieser Karte nach den Bestimmungen für Wochenkarten zur Fahrt auf der in der Karte bezeichneten Strecke und nur an den aus dem Wertschein ersichtlichen Tagen berechtigt.

Die Karte ist ohne Unterschrift oder ohne Paßbild ungültig. Sie ist den Schaffnern und Aufsichtsbeamten unaufgefordert u. offen auszuhändigen.

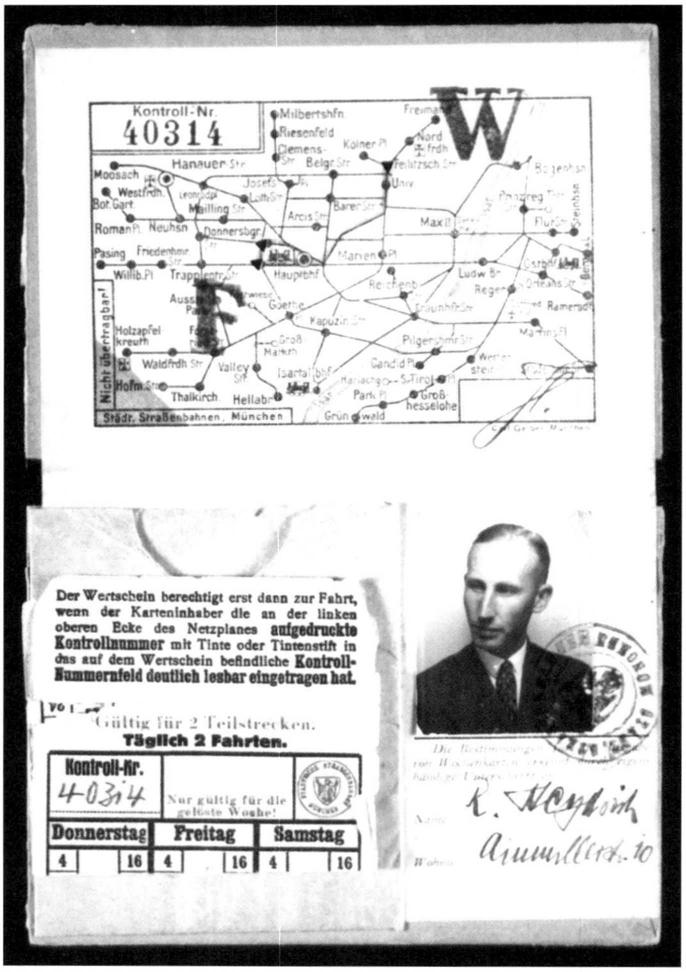

Kontroll-Nr. 40314

Nicht übertragbar!

Städt. Straßenbahnen, München

Der Wertschein berechtigt erst dann zur Fahrt, wenn der Karteninhaber die an der linken oberen Ecke des Netzplanes **aufgedruckte Kontrollnummer** mit Tinte oder Tintenstift in das auf dem Wertschein befindliche **Kontroll-Nummernfeld deutlich lesbar eingetragen hat.**

Gültig für 2 Teilstrecken.

Täglich 2 Fahrten.

Kontroll-Nr. 40314

Nur gültig für die gelöste Woche!

Donnerstag		Freitag		Samstag	
4	16	4	16	4	16

Name R. Heydrich

Wohnung Ainmillerstr. 10

Heydrich's street car pass showing his address at Ainmillerstrasse 10. The pass survived the war, and to date remains in an English collection.

Wittlesbacher Palace, Munich, became the new offices for Reichsführer-SS Himmler as Chief of the Bavarian Police.

Wittlesbacher Palace, Munich, interior office. Of interest is the photograph of Adolf Wagner the Bavarian Minister, to the wall and the SS runes decoration above the far window.

A WORKING DAY FOR THE SECURITY CHIEF

One of the few occasions that Heydrich could take a leisurely working breakfast, usually coffee at the office would have to suffice.

At work in his office at the Wittlesbacher Palace, Heydrich hears news from his adjutant. A photograph of Reichsführer-SS Himmler can be seen above the bookcase.

As with most Security Chiefs throughout the world, paperwork took up most of the time. An ashtray can be seen on the desk top, Heydrich was an occasional smoker.

members were being flown other than that of the new German Government. His complaint was ignored. Determined to show this 'nation of inn-keepers' that the National Socialists were not to be toyed with, he arranged with SD agents in Geneva to obtain a giant blood-red swastika flag which one night was promptly secured to the roof of the hotel. The following morning, all Geneva knew who held the reins of power in Germany. Ambassador Nadolny promptly sent Heydrich home!

This prank displayed the youthful inexperience of the head of the fledgling security service. In mentioning his escapades, Lina states, *"At that age one can't expect wisdom. Once, he jumped into the water in full uniform in order to recover a handkerchief belonging to me that I had accidentally dropped into the Starnberger See".* One must remember that he was only thirty-eight at his death and Himmler had been only twenty-nine when he took control of the SS. Generally, the higher echelons of the SS organisation were made up of very young men.

The Himmler-Heydrich partnership realised that true power rested in the capital and Heydrich was despatched on 15th March 1933 to visit Berlin, where the SS was controlled by Kurt Daluege, a former refuse engineer. Daluege had been given the command of the uniform police in Prussia and was appointed Ministerial Director in the Prussian Ministry of the Interior. He had a rather vacant look about him, resulting in the nickname 'Dummi Dummi'. The truth however was different, Daluege was not slow to recognise his powerful position and, although he held junior rank to Himmler in the SS, he noted an 'envious eye' looking at him from the Bavarian capital. Heydrich installed himself in the Berlin Savoy Hotel near the Zoo and attempted to see SS-Gruppenführer Daluege. Heydrich's efforts were in vain, Daluege had no wish to see the upstart from Munich who could only have instructions from the Reichsführer that would interfere with his own plans. The telephonists at the Ministry of the Interior were informed not to put calls through from the young visitor. After several days, Heydrich, filled with rage and indignation at the rebuff, wrote to Daluege,

SS-Gruppenführer
Kurt Daluege

> *"Since Thursday I have been trying without success to penetrate the protective screen. I have telephoned no less than six times. Since I have to travel back today, I beg you to recognise this as a token of my visit and hope that the opportunity for a personal visit will present itself in about ten days. I remain your most humble and obedient servant, R. Heydrich. Heil Hitler!"* [12]

These were some of the problems that faced the young Heydrich, Himmler and the embryo SS. It was going to take a few more years before the SS organisation as a whole held undisputed power within the NSDAP. Himmler was installed as Chief of the Bavarian Political Police on 1st April and Heydrich exercised power on his behalf. Himmler and Heydrich still gazed northwards and planned to extricate the power they sought from the grasp of their Prussian associates. First, however, they built up their own power base before grabbing at other sources of authority.

The Bavarian Minister of the Interior, Adolf Wagner, directed Himmler to take control of 'all political sections of the state police authorities and police offices, all political police sections in local government, district offices and municipalities and all formations of the political auxiliary police for the executive; the concentration camps, whether already in existence or still to be established '[13]. This was the birth of what was later to be termed as the 'SS State.' Heydrich's staff grew rapidly in numbers.

Heinrich Müller

Franz Josef Huber

The SD chief sacked all politically opposing police officials down to the lowest levels; incompetent officers were also shown the door. Two names that came under his scrutiny were later to become important to his story. Police Inspectors Heinrich Müller and Franz Josef Huber were employed in the Political Section of the Munich Police. Both

Bayerische Politische Polizei

B. Nr...
(Stets bei Antwort anzugeben)

München, den 12. April 1934
Fernsprecher 28 3 41

1940

An

Reichsführer SS.

Betrifft: Polizeidirektion Ludwigshafen.
Vorgang:

Staatsanwalt Dr. S t e p p beim Bayer. Staatsministeriu der Justiz ist als Leiter der Polizeidirektion Ludwigshafen ausersehen. Dr. Stepp ist langjähriger Parteigenosse, erprobter Nationalsozialist und hat als Verbindungsmann zwischen Bayer. Staatsministerium der Justiz und Bayer. Politischen Polizei sich so hervorragende Verdienste erworben, daß diese seine Beförderung zum Standartenführer gerechtfertigt erscheinen lassen. Es wird daher gebeten, Dr. Stepp zum Standartenführer zu befördern, damit er als zukünftiger Leiter der Polizeidirektion Ludwigshafen einen den übrigen Parteidienststellen der Pfalz entsprechenden Rang bekleidet.

Heydrich

Der Politische Polizeikommandeur Nr. 166			16.IV.34					Anlagen
Abt.	Kdr.	Ad.	P.Pol.	P.H.Pol.	W.A.	4.5.34		
an	16.IV.34	16.IV.34						—
ab	16.IV.34	16.IV.34						
gez.		H4.						

Document dated 12th April 1934 and sent from Heydrich to Reichsführer-SS Himmler. The document bears the new 'Bayerische Politische Polizei' (Bavarian Political Police) heading and is dated just 11 days after Himmler took over this office. Heydrich details an assessment of Dr.Stepp.

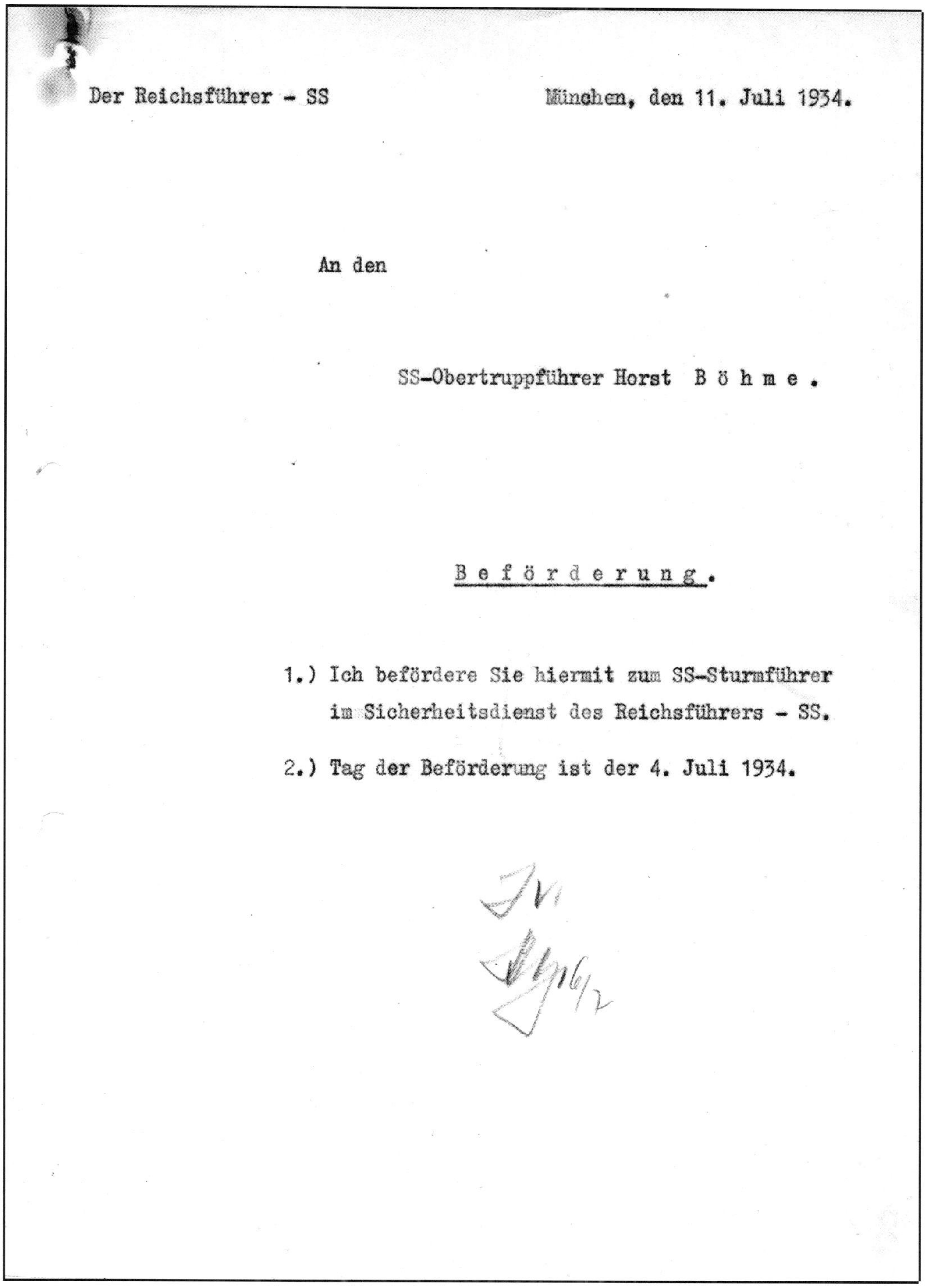

Der Reichsführer - SS

München, den 11. Juli 1934.

An den

SS-Obertruppführer Horst B ö h m e .

B e f ö r d e r u n g .

1.) Ich befördere Sie hiermit zum SS-Sturmführer im Sicherheitsdienst des Reichsführers - SS.

2.) Tag der Beförderung ist der 4. Juli 1934.

Document dated 11th July 1934 and signed by Heydrich in red pencil. By June 1934 the SD became the only official intelligence service within the Party. This document promotes SS-Obertruppführer Horst Böhme to SS-Sturmführer with the SD, Böhme became the Security Police Commander in Prague and subsequently commanded an Einsatz Kommando in Russia.

SS-Oberführer Reinhard Heydrich arrives in his car accompanied by SS-Standartenführer Aumeier (*the leader of the 47th Standarte and one of Himmler's first personal adjutants*) sometime in 1933. The photographer captures a sinister gaze from the young Security Chief.

The Munich Police Headquarters at Ettstrasse. It was here that Heydrich marched in at the head of a troop of SS men. Two policemen, both opposers of the NSDAP, Heinrich Müller and Franz Josef Huber, were going to resist the Security Chief. Huber was immediately sacked by Heydrich but later re-instated. Both he and Müller moved their allegiance to the NSDAP and eventually attained high positions within the SS.

were supporters of the Bavarian People's Party, directly opposed to the NSDAP. Müller related that he and Huber were prepared to physically resist Heydrich when he arrived at the Police HQ in Ettstrasse at the head of a troop of SS men during the seizure of power [14]. The fact that Müller had not been previously active against the National Socialists was his saving grace . Huber was sacked, but then summoned to see Heydrich and reinstated. Heydrich knew he needed men of high professional ability like Müller and Huber, and as long as they did not constitute a security risk, he was prepared to overlook their previous political leanings. Müller was later to attain the rank of SS-Gruppenführer with command of Department IV in the 'RSHA' [15]. Huber became a SS-Brigadeführer and was Chief of the Security Police and SD in Vienna [16].

It was Heydrich's intention, now the National Socialists were running the show, to consolidate power for the SS and prevent it becoming another SA, which, from within the SS, were concidered an undisciplined rabble. Heydrich's widow, was later to confirm that he murmured deliriously on his deathbed, *"The stupid SA, the stupid SA "* [17]. Any fears Heydrich had of the SS becoming another SA were unfounded, and by the following year, the SS would be released from it's present SA control. Meanwhile Heydrich had much to do, breaking any opposition to the NSDAP.

Given the powers by the emergency decree following the Reichstag fire in 1933, Heydrich began to arrest the political opposition, including trade union officials, communists, Jews and any other person who displayed tendencies considered hostile to the state. The prisons became over crowded and Wagner suggested to Hans Frank, the Justice Minister, that camps should be set up to take the pressure off the prisons. The concentration camp system in Germany was born. The British had operated similar establishments in South Africa during the Boer War, but it would be the German version that would stay in the minds of people forever. Heydrich has often been credited with their creation, but the Israeli historian, Shlomo Aronson, has traced the original idea and placed it firmly at the feet of Adolf Wagner [18].

On 22nd March 1933 the first official camp opened just outside Munich in a small town called Dachau. It's commander was SS-Oberführer Hilmar Wäckerle [19]. He ran a brutal regime and complaints were soon streaming into the office of the Reichsführer from all directions. Murders were committed by the camp guards and soon Wäckerle became an embarrassment. He was promptly replaced by SS-Oberführer Theodore Eicke who immediately re-organised the camp system and created a set of regulations that would form the basis of rules for all the future camps [20].

Hilmar Wäckerle
First Commandant of Dachau
Concentration Camp

Theodor Eicke
Took over command of Dachau
from Wäckerle

Heydrich's SD held sway over who was admitted to the camp and who was released, but what happened inside was left to Eicke. This was to prove a sticking point for Heydrich throughout his career. Persons arrested were detained under the phrase 'protective custody' and in those early years, detention was generally for a short period. In the month of July 1933, 2097 people were detained and 1820 were released. For the whole of 1933, a total of 16409 persons were arrested under protective custody orders and 12554 were released [21]. At this stage, Jews were only arrested for political activities. One man was even arrested for paying his factory workers at a rate of pay below that recommended by the government. Wilhelm Frick, the Reich Minister of the Interior, complained to Himmler that too many prisoners were being arrested in Bavaria compared to the remainder of the Reich, but his remonstrations fell upon deaf ears. Himmler and Heydrich intended to use Bavaria as a testing ground for their future dream of a Reich Police Force, controlled by the SS.

Was this concept thought up by Heydrich or Himmler? Lina had no doubt that it was her husband's idea: *"My husband forced the idea of the Reich Police on Himmler. He was always shoving Himmler along in front of himself." She continued, "He knew that without Himmler he would be completely written off as far as the circle of Munich putsch veterans was concerned "* [22]. Former SD officer Höttl also agreed post-war with Lina's view [23].

Meanwhile, the Himmler-Heydrich partnership had not forgotten Berlin. Hermann Göring controlled the Prussian Police which included the police of the Reich capital. Within this framework, the Prussian Political

Police had been placed under the command of one Rudolf Diels who acted on behalf of Göring (and was married to Göring's cousin). He re-organised the department and moved it's centre of operations to a former Berlin art school situated at Prinz Albrecht Strasse 8. In April, Göring made Diels' department a special state authority answerable to only himself. It was then christened the "Secret State Police Headquarters" or "Gestapa" for short. On it's staff was a police Hauptmann, Arthur Nebe who had connections with Himmler and Heydrich in Munich, his loyalty to them was later rewarded. Realising that some concessions had to be made to his opposite numbers in Bavaria, Göring agreed on the appointment of a liaison man between the SS High Command and his Gestapa. Himmler decided on a Heydrich SD man for the job and SS-Hauptsturmführer Heinz Jost was nominated. Göring now believed that he had satisfied Himmler and boasted, *"Himmler and Heydrich will never get to Berlin "* [24]. Things did look disheartening for our two SS men, but events were to take a strange turn when support arrived from an unexpected source.

Wilhelm Frick, as Reich Minister of the Interior, also wanted to see a police structure in Germany under one authority. Naturally, he thought this should be his Interior Ministry. In November 1933, Göring removed the Gestapa from the control of the Ministry of the Interior, a move that would drive Frick to confrontation since he did not have his own power base within the Party. Reich Minister Frick had been quick to realise that Himmler would support him against Göring, but he also considered, incorrectly, that he could control Himmler. Frick assisted Himmler to take control of the Political Police in Lübeck, Hamburg, Baden and Württemberg,

Göring hands over control of the Gestapa to the Reichsführer-SS Heinrich Himmler, April 1934

Rudolf Diels
Diels was in command of the Prussian Political Police under Göring

Heinz Jost
The liaison man between the SS and Göring's Gestapa, before Himmler took over control

Dr.Wilhelm Frick
Reichminister of the Interior

SS-Gruppenführer Reinhard Heydrich

Formal portrait of the Security Chief, taken in late 1936, early 1937.
Heydrich was promoted to SS-Gruppenführer on the 30th June 1934

Two formal portraits of SS-Gruppenführer Heydrich, the upper portrait shows him in the black service tunic while the lower portrait by Hoffmann shows him in the new field grey uniform.

Der Reichsführer SS

München, den 24.Dezember 1933.

Herrn

SS-Brigadeführer H e y d r i c h

Ich schenke Ihnen den Totenkopfring der SS.

Er soll sein:

Ein Zeichen unserer Treue zum Führer, unseres unwandelbaren Gehorsams gegen unsere Vorgesetzten und unserer unerschütterlichen Zusammengehörigkeit und Kameradschaft.

Der Totenkopf ist die Mahnung, jederzeit bereit zu sein, das Leben unseres Ichs einzusetzen für das Leben der Gesamtheit.

Die Runen dem Totenkopf gegenüber sind Heilszeichen unserer Vergangenheit, mit der wir durch die Weltanschauung des Nationalsozialismus erneut verbunden sind.

Die beiden Sig-Runen versinnbilden den Namen unserer Schutzstaffel.

Hakenkreuz und Hagall-Rune sollen uns den nicht zu erschütternden Glauben an den Sieg unserer Weltanschauung vor Augen halten.

Umkränzt ist der Ring von Eichenlaub, den Blättern des alten deutschen Baumes.

Dieser Ring ist käuflich nicht erwerbbar und darf nie in fremde Hände kommen.

Mit Ihrem Ausscheiden aus der SS oder aus dem Leben geht dieser Ring zurück an den Reichsführer SS.

Abbildungen und Nachahmungen sind strafbar und Sie haben dieselben zu verhüten.

Tragen Sie den Ring in Ehren!

H. Himmler

The citation for Heydrich's Totenkopfring awarded on the 24th December 1933 and signed in ink by Reichsführer-SS Himmler. The Heydrich ring citation turned up at auction in England during the 1980's but was withdrawn from the sale due to it being inadvertantly torn in half. To date it's location is unknown.

Heydrich was one of the very first recipients of the new SS-Totenkopfring.The ring was going to assist in establishing a new religious base to the SS and was owned by the recipient until their death, after which it was returned to the SS where it would be taken to be enshrined within the Wewelsburg Castle. It is believed that Heydrich's ring was given personally to Reichsführer-SS Himmler after his death and was taken by Himmler to Wewelsburg Castle. Russel , the author of 'Heinrich Himmler's Burg' (Heitz & Hoffkes 1989) has found evidence that there was a'Heydrich Room' set up at Wewelsburg Castle by Himmler after Heydrich's death. This being the case, it seems plausible the ring may have been placed there.

Preußische Geheime Staatspolizei
Der Stellvertretende Chef

B.-Nr. 606/37 – I A

Bitte in der Antwort vorstehendes Geschäftszeichen und Datum anzugeben.

Berlin SW 11, den 27. März 1937
Prinz-Albrecht-Straße 8
Fernsprecher: A 2 Flora 0040

An
Herrn Polizeiinspektor
Wilhelm L u d w i g
im H a u s e
Abteilung II

Im Einvernehmen mit dem Herrn Reichs- und Preußischen Minister des Innern habe ich Sie zum P o l i z e i - O b e r i n s p e k t o r ernannt. Gleichzeitig verleihe ich Ihnen mit Wirkung vom 1. Februar 1937 ab eine Polizei-Oberinspektorstelle der Besoldungsgruppe 4 b 2 (Endgrundgehalt 5500.- RM) bei dem Geheimen Staatspolizeiamt in Berlin.

Wegen Berechnung und Anweisung der erhöhten Bezüge wird das Referat I C das Weitere veranlassen.

In Vertretung:

Document dated 27th March 1937, with the 'Preusische Geheime Staatspolizei' (Prussian Secret State Police) heading. Heydrich was operating from the Prinz-Albrecht-Strasse in Berlin, when he signed this document in his capacity as 'Deputy Chief'. The document officially promoted a 'Polizei-inspektor' (Police Inspector) to 'Polizei-oberinspektor' (Police Inspector 1st Rating) within the Gestapo.

Im Namen des Reichs!

Ich ernenne den Kriminalassistenten

Richard L i p p o l d

zum Kriminalsekretär im Reichsdienst.

Ich vollziehe diese Urkunde in der Erwartung, daß der Ernannte getreu seinem Diensteide seine Amtspflichten gewissenhaft erfüllt und das Vertrauen rechtfertigt, das ihm durch diese Ernennung bewiesen wird. Zugleich darf er des besonderen Schutzes des Führers und Reichskanzlers sicher sein.

Berlin, den 19. April 1937.

Namens des Führers und Reichskanzlers.
Für den Ministerpräsidenten
Der Stellvertretende Chef
der Preußischen Geheimen Staatspolizei.

In Vertretung:

B.Nr. 3516/37 I E.

This official citation promotion of ' Kriminalassistenten' (Criminal Assistant) Richard Lippold to 'Krim nalsekretär' (Criminal Secretary) has been signed by Heydrich on the19th April 1937, one day before Hitler's birthday. The document displays the relief wreathed eagle with swastika and the ink signature of Heydrich in his capacity as Deputy Chief of the Prussian Secret State Police.

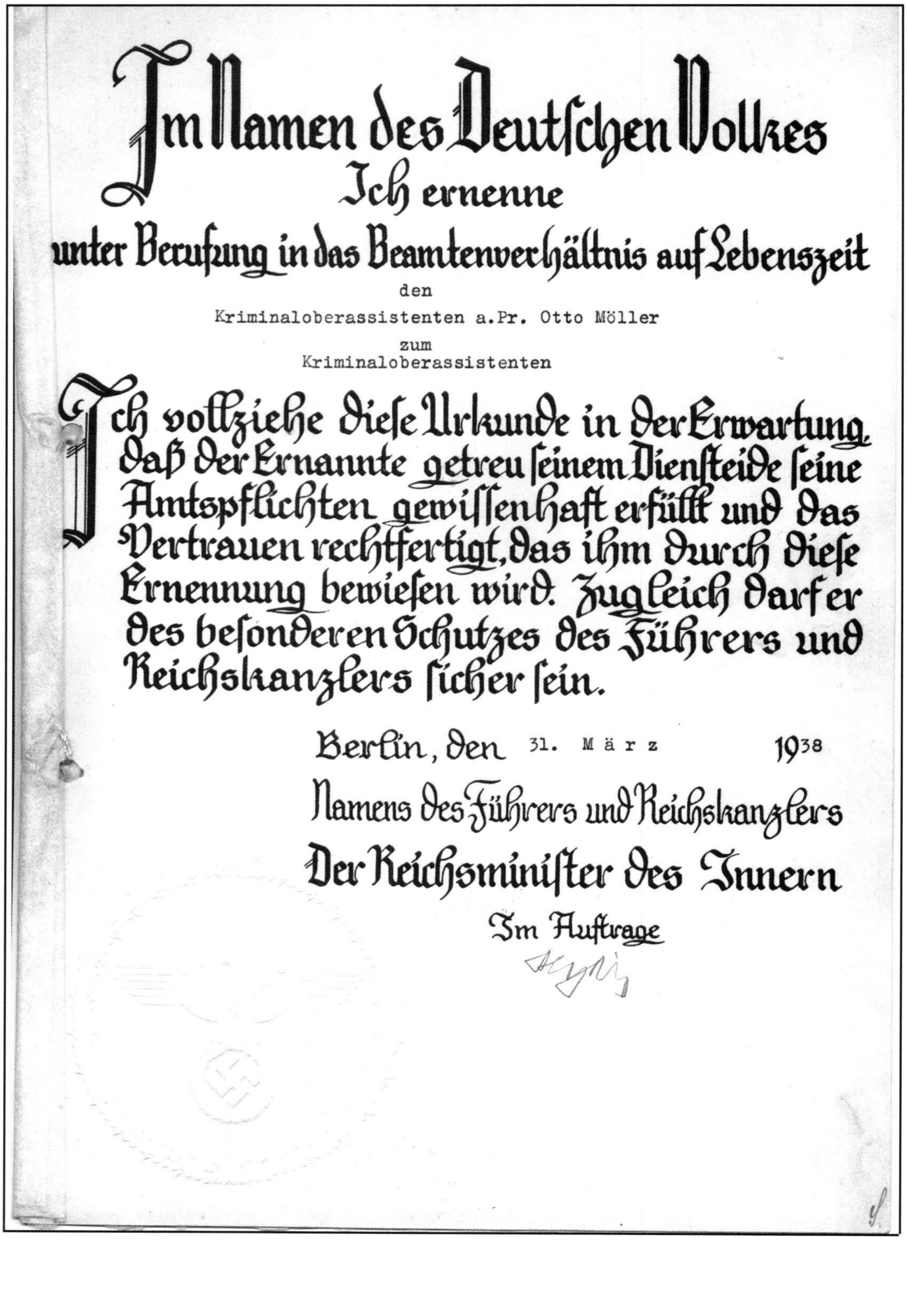

Im Namen des Deutschen Volkes

Ich ernenne

unter Berufung in das Beamtenverhältnis auf Lebenszeit

den

Kriminaloberassistenten a.Pr. Otto Möller

zum

Kriminaloberassistenten

Ich vollziehe diese Urkunde in der Erwartung, daß der Ernannte getreu seinem Diensteide seine Amtspflichten gewissenhaft erfüllt und das Vertrauen rechtfertigt, das ihm durch diese Ernennung bewiesen wird. Zugleich darf er des besonderen Schutzes des Führers und Reichskanzlers sicher sein.

Berlin, den 31. März 1938

Namens des Führers und Reichskanzlers

Der Reichsminister des Innern

Im Auftrage

A formal promotion citation signed in ink by Heydrich on the 31st March 1938, shortly after the annexation of Austria with Germany. The citation is signed on behalf of the 'Führer und Reichskanzlers' and the Reichsminister of the Interior.

Der Reichsführer SS
Der Chef des Sicherheitshauptamtes

I 112
43 - 14

Berlin, d. 26.FEB.1936

An
den SA-Gruppenführer Südwest,
Gruppenführer L u d i n,

S t u t t g a r t.

Lieber Kamerad Ludin !

Ihren Brief vom 21.Januar 1936 bestätigend, teile ich Ihnen mit, dass ich grundsätzlich einer Übernahme von SA-Führern und Männern der SA-Hilfswerklager in den Sicherheitsdienst nicht entgegenstehe. Augenblicklich ist es aber aus etatmässigen Gründen überhaupt nicht möglich, eine Erweiterung unseres Personalbestandes vorzunehmen und wir müssen sogar dem Vernehmen nach mit einer Beschränkung unseres uns zur Verfügung stehenden Etats im kommenden Jahre rechnen. Sollten sich die diesbezüglichen Verhältnisse im Laufe der nächsten Monate gebessert haben, so werde ich Bewerbungen von ehemaligen Angehörigen der Hilfswerklager von Fall zu Fall entscheiden, so wie dies auch bei Übernahme von Angehörigen anderer Organisationen bisher geschehen ist.
Zu meinem Bedauern bin ich daher im Augenblick nicht in der Lage, Ihrer Bitte zu entsprechen.

Heil Hitler !

SS - Gruppenführer.

Letter dated 26th February 1936 from Heydrich to SA- Gruppenführer Ludin. Heydrich in reply to Ludin's letter of the21st January states that although in principle he is not opposed to accepting officers and men from the SA into the Security Service, their budget for expansion of personnel will not allow for further recruitment at that time. Heydrich goes on to say that he is expecting a reduction in their budget for the following year which will also stop any further expansion. Interestingly, Ludin is trying to get SA personnel into the Security Service while Heydrich is politely refusing. If it was indeed a question of budget or simply that SA personnel were not wanted by Heydrich within the Security Service isn't known. Suffice to say much of Heydrich's recruitment drive was aimed at young professionals especially with legal backgrounds. In all probability many of the SA membership would not have fitted Heydrich's criteria.

Josef Meisinger

Werner Best

Günther Patschowsky

Gerhard Flesch

THE NEW GESTAPO ASSISTANTS

THE NEW SD 'INTELLECTUALS'

The SD attracted many lawyers and intellectuals. These were precisely the type of applicants to the security service that Heydrich was looking for.

Walter Schellenburg

Otto Ohlendorf

Hermann Behrends

Franz Six

Anhalt, Bremen, Thüringen and Hesse. By January 1934 Braunschweig, Oldenburg and Sachsen were to follow [25]. These moves placed Himmler in command of all the Political Police Forces throughout the Reich, with the exception of the largest, Prussia. Göring now realised that he could not prevent the Himmler-Heydrich team rolling into Berlin, so he decided to negotiate with Frick and Himmler.

During this time, Heydrich's SD uncovered a plot to assassinate the Minister President of Prussia. Heydrich immediately recognised the significance of this discovery. Had Diels' own intelligence service failed to uncover the plot? Surely this would display the superiority of the SD over Göring's own Gestapa and place him under an obligation of deep gratitude. Göring caved in, but still made vain attempts to retain some element of control, even if in name only. Diels was removed to a government post in the Rhineland and Himmler was named Inspector of the Secret State Police. On 22nd April 1934, Heydrich was rewarded with the task of directing the Gestapa. Müller, Huber and Flesch moved to Berlin [26].

Heydrich immediately set about re-organisation. The name 'Gestapo' was introduced. The term 'adviser' was replaced by 'adjutant' and all was placed upon a much more military footing. Dr. Werner Best, an SD man, was given charge of Administration, Organisation, and Law in Division I. Heydrich retained control of Division II, but drew upon the expertise of both Müller and Flesch. Josef Meisinger was given the job of observing his own Party and its organisations. Division III, Counter Espionage, was given to Dr. Günther Patschowsky, a SD colleague from pre-1933 days and therefore it remained under the firm control of the Chief [27]. Heydrich's staff not only admired him, but in some respects feared him, for he possessed a remarkable memory, remembering all telephone and file numbers plus explicit detail of events going back some months previous.

Similarities existed between the SD and the Gestapo that would remain and cause confusion until the introduction of the Reich Central Security Department in 1939. Many staff were employed by both departments and areas of responsibility often overlapped. The SD counted among its staff some of the top intelligentsia of the country. They were obviously keen to work in some capacity for the new State, but the prospect of the SA or the Party did not compare with the intrigue of the SD, along with its prestigious black SS uniform. Heydrich was keen to attract lawyers and these included such names as the aforementioned Werner Best, Hermann Behrends and Otto Ohlendorf. Other intellectuals willingly drawn into the net included the university professor Franz Six, plus the jurist and political scientist, Walter Schellenberg.

On 21st March 1933, Heydrich was promoted to SS-Oberführer on the Staff of the Reichsführer-SS [28]. That summer, he had been given back control of the SD and on 9th November 1933, he was promoted to the rank of SS-Brigadeführer [29]. Simultaneously, the SD was officially recognised as the fifth SS Branch [30]. In June 1934, the SD was ordered by the Fuhrer's Deputy, Rudolf Hess, to be the only official intelligence service within the Party [31] and Heydrich's achievements received further recognition by his promotion to SS-Gruppenführer on 30th June [32]. Late in November or December that year, the SD headquarters offices moved to the Prinz Albrecht Palace in Berlin at Wilhelmstrasse 102. Heydrich had arrived in Berlin [33].

The SS and Gestapo Headquarters at Prinz-Albrecht-Strasse 8, Berlin, the former old art school building

Main hallway within the Prinz-Albrecht-Strasse 8, Berlin. A bust of Hitler stands to the viewers right and one of Göring to the left.

Prinz Albrecht Palace at Wilhelmstrasse 102, Berlin. This became the SD headquarters from 1934 and remained it's headquarters until 1945.

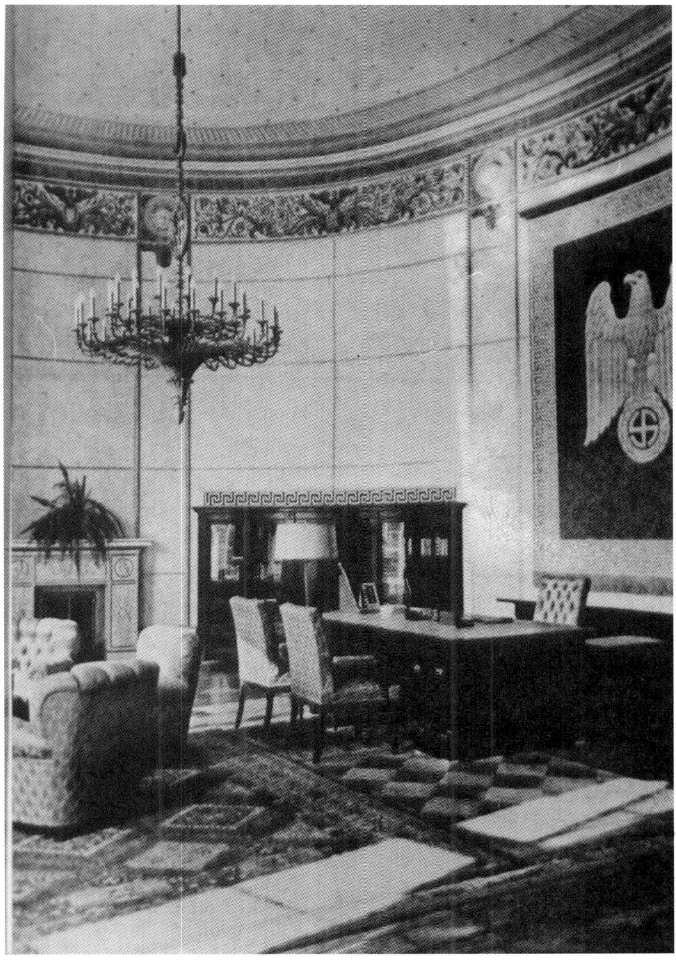

The personal office of the Security Chief SS-Gruppenführer Reinhard Heydrich within the Prinz Albrecht Palace. A remarkable tapestry featuring an eagle clutching a wreathed Sunwheel Swastika hung directly behind his desk.

it's readers. Subsequently, d'Alquen was placed on the staff of Heydrich's SD. Heydrich wrote many articles, some anonymously, often attacking the Church, which he declared was creating distrust in the mission of the Führer. He also highlighted the moral and cultural corruption in the Church leadership, citing sex scandals and financial dishonesty [15]. The Jews came off lightly, Streicher being left to spearhead that attack in his 'Der Stürmer'. Heydrich would often attack the Italians, whom he saw as pawns of the Church of Rome. His anti-Italian stance over the invasion of Abyssinia is particularly ironic, given that the 'Duce' was to become Hitler's strongest ally.

Elsewhere, the one-time ally of Himmler and Heydrich, Minister of the Interior Wilhelm Frick, now took his opportunity to try and restrict the power of the Reichsführer-SS. Frick had not lost his dream of a united German Police under his control. Several of the old Party hierarchy saw the Himmler-Heydrich partnership as gaining too much strength. In particular, the anti-SS Gauleiter, Erich Koch, complained to Frick about the Gestapo agents operating in his sphere of authority. As a result, a new Gestapo law was introduced on 10th February 1936 which included the paragraph 'Gestapo Stellen' (Gestapo Departments) are, at the same time, subordinate to the relevant 'Regierungspräsident' (Local Government President), will conform to his instructions and will keep him informed of all political police matters [16].

Himmler saw this as a concession for which he desired recompense. He demanded the Ministry formulate a law incorporating the different branches of the police into one Reich Police Force. Frick agreed, but his vision differed from that of Himmler. He intended the new police organisation should be kept in his hands as Reichsminister and he saw Kurt Daluege as his chief of police. He had not reckoned on the powerful Himmler-Heydrich partnership which had allied itself with it's old foe Göring. Not surprisingly, Himmler rejected Frick's proposal. On 9th June 1936, Heydrich presented their counter-proposals and declared that Hitler wished to see Himmler installed as Chief of the German Police. Heydrich proposed:-

1. A Chief of German Police will be appointed who will be charged with handling all police affairs which come under the jurisdiction of the Reich Minister of the Interior.
2. Heinrich Himmler will be appointed "Reichsführer-SS and Chief of the German Police". He will be answerable personally to the Reich Minister of the Interior and to the Prussian Minister of the Interior.
3. The Chief of the German Police will hold the rank of Reich Minister and will be a member of the Reich cabinet [17].

An angry Frick went straight to see Hitler who calmed his minister, but pressed him to agree, with one concession. Himmler's cabinet rank was rejected. Frick still attempted to have the title 'Reichsführer-SS' deleted from the new designation, but Heydrich stood his ground successfully.

Hitler's decree on 17th June 1936, appointed Himmler to the new post of 'Reichsführer-SS and Chief of German Police' [18]. The jubilant Himmler immediately demonstrated his interpretation of the new position. He divided the Police into the Security Police and the Order Police. Heydrich received his just reward with control of the Security Police. This department included the entire Secret State Police, the Criminal Police, the Frontier Police and the Counter-Espionage Police. The defeated Frick candidate, Daluege, inherited the left-overs. This, in the Order Police Department, included the Traffic Police, the Protection Police or ordinary police and the Police Administration [19].

Heydrich had now attained more power than any policeman before him and even his successor, Kaltenbrunner, did not wield the same influence. Only the concentration camp administration eluded him. He had power of detention and release, but no authority over what went on inside the camps and he saw this as a hindrance. Himmler, however, had recognised the accumulation of power that his young subordinate had accrued and had no intention of allowing Heydrich yet another inroad into his own authority. He promptly appointed SS-Brigadeführer Theodore Eicke as Inspector of Concentration Camps [20], much to the annoyance of his security chief. With responsibility direct to Himmler, 'Papa' Eicke's situation was unassailable and he often took advantage of his unique position.

Reichsführer-SS Himmler now had control of the police, and his SS organisation had moved from a small subsidiary of the SA into the most powerful organ of the Third Reich. The future would view Hitler's time in office through the eyes of the new 'Black Order'.

CHAPTER 7
FOUNDATION OF THE SS STATE

On 17th June 1933, Lina Heydrich went into labour in Berlin, her husband assisted the doctor with the home delivery and the proud parents were soon able to announce the arrival of a healthy baby boy, whom they named Klaus [1].

At about the time of the accession to power in Prussia, Himmler moved from his smallholding at Munich-Waldtrudering to a larger house in Gmund on the Tegernsee. The area is still a beautiful spot that attracts annual visitors to the lake shore towns, many of whom are unaware of the significance of a previous occupier. The Heydrichs also planned a move, but this time it was not to the quiet countryside of Bavaria, but the centre of political activity, Berlin. With the intention of a summer move they found suitable accommodation in the Berlin suburb of Südende, however the events of June-July 1934 prevented their move from taking place. Heydrich was able to arrange temporary accommodation for his family at the Prinz Albrecht Strasse, Lina did not see her husband for days and only communicated by telephone. He informed her of the Röhm revolt (understanding this was difficult for her to appreciate since Röhm had been their son's godfather) and the subsequent events.

The details of the 'Night of Long Knives' are well documented, but mention must be made here of Heydrich's participation. He has been cited by many witnesses as a 'major player' in those events. The old family friend, Karl von Eberstein, declared post-war that Heydrich assisted in drawing up the execution list and must be held responsible for many of the deeds of that night and the following days. Von Eberstein declares that, in his area of responsibility, Dresden, eight executions by firing squad were carried out, but the SD man, SS-Obersturmbannführer Beutel, had a 'Sonderauftrag' (special instruction) from Heydrich to shoot about twenty-eight people [2].

There are tales of Göring, Himmler, Körner and Heydrich closeting themselves in a room, the door opening and closing as orders were issued from within for the execution of various individuals. There can be little or no doubt that old scores were settled during those hours. Serious historical scholars must agree that little documentary evidence survives this episode and the actual events are open to conjecture, however, there is evidence that Heydrich was ultimately responsible for the execution of the leader of the 'Catholic Action Group', Dr. Erich Klausener [3].

Police Superintendent Josef Meisinger had been delegated responsibility for the observation of Klausener and his group. Klausener, Daluege's predecessor as head of the police division in the Prussian Ministry of the Interior, had made plain his opposition to the new regime. Göring had replaced him with Daluege and moved him to the Ministry of Transport. His leadership of Catholic Action had brought him to the attention of the SD Chief. Legal measures against Klausener had failed to silence him and he continued to take every opportunity to speak out against the National Socialist government at public meetings to the point of acute embarrassment. At a meeting of the Catholics at the Hoppegarten on 24th June, Klausener voiced strong opinions 'against the interests of the State', hence, on the fateful day of 30th June, Heydrich allegedly ordered SS-Hauptsturmführer Kurt Gildisch to *"take over Klausener's case and shoot him yourself"* [4]. Gildisch duly obliged, shooting Klausener in his office. He then telephoned his boss who ordered him to make the deed appear as suicide. Gildisch later stood trial in 1957 for the murder of Klausener and confirmed Göring's version of events given at Nuremberg. Following this successful mission, Gildisch was despatched to Bremen where he was also responsible for the arrest of SA-Gruppenführer Karl Ernst as he prepared to depart on his honeymoon. Ernst was returned to the Lichterfelde SS barracks in Berlin and executed.

With this purge, Hitler and his associates had removed nearly all dangerous opposition, including such names as Gregor Strasser, General von Schleicher, General Kurt von Bredow, Fritz Gerlich and many others. Revenge was exacted for the failed 'beerhall' putsch of November 1923. Gustav von Kahr and Otto von Lossow were both assassinated. The Vice Chancellor, Franz von Papen, only just escaped death. No less than twelve Reichstag Deputies disappeared during that weekend, every one a senior SA leader. Röhm, the SA Chief of Staff, was shot in his Stadelheim Prison cell by Theodore Eicke and his adjutant, Michael Lippert [5]. Röhm had refused Hitler's offer of a pistol for suicide, protesting his innocence and loyalty to the last, he died with the words *"Mein Führer, mein Führer"* on his lips. Among the other senior SA leaders to perish were Heines, Hayn, Schneidhuber, von Heydebreck, Kasche, von Krauser, Schmidt, Count von Spreti and Schragmüller [6]. The evening newspapers of 30th June simply announced the replacement of Röhm by Viktor Lutze. On 13th July, Hitler reported in his speech to the Reichstag that seventy-seven

THE RÖHM PUTSCH OF 1934, HEYDRICH'S PART

Heydrich was heavily involved in the Röhm Putsch.

Both Eicke and Lippert were involved in the execution of SA Stabschef Röhm.

SS-Hauptsturmführer Gildisch shot the leader of the Catholic Action Group, Dr.Erich Klausener, allegedly on Heydrich's orders.

SA Stabschef Röhm

Karl Ernst

Dr.Erich Klausener leader of the Catholic Action Group.

Gregor Strasser

General von Schleicher

RÖHM, ERNST, KLAUSENER, STRASSER AND VON SCHLEICHER WERE JUST A FEW OF THOSE THAT FELL VICTIM IN THE SO CALLED 'RÖHM PUTSCH'

people had perished [7]. No other official figure exists, but this estimate must be below the actual total. By special decree on 26th July 1934, Hitler formally removed the SS from SA supervision. Henceforth, the SS became an independent organisation, making Himmler accountable to Hitler alone [8].

On 2nd August 1934, the aged Hindenburg died. Hitler at once moved to take absolute control, supported by his Minister of Defence, General von Blomberg. The Army Commander-in-Chief, Generaloberst von Fritsch, opposed Hitler's aim at the Presidency. The Führer gained the confidence of the armed forces and introduced an oath of allegiance, sworn personally to him by name. Von Fritsch admitted defeat and united with his colleagues behind the new Chancellor and Führer of the German Reich.

Shortly after the Röhm Putsch, Lina visited her parents at their old family home in Fehmarn, she had longed for a home in the country. Where better than the island of her upbringing? On her return, she pestered her husband for a second home on the island and he finally relented, agreeing to the building of a summer house. The problem then arose of how to finance such a dream, salvation came in the form of the Consul, Willy Sachs who loaned the Heydrichs the necessary funds (the mortgage agreement apparently still exists in the offices of the land registry in the town of Burg). A friend of the family, an architect and SS-Sturmführer Gustav Rall, designed the house [9] which grew from the original idea into a large building. A second mortgage was required and final payment of the loan of 42,000 Reichsmarks was to become due in 1952. Building work began in the spring of 1935 and, on completion in June, a great mid-summer celebration was held. The Reichsführer attended and presented the new home with a hand made blacksmith's door lock, which now rests in the home of a well known German historian [10]. Heydrich arranged his leave to coincide with the move into the new house.

A second son, Heider, was born on 23rd December 1934, the SS-Gruppenführer was well satisfied with his wife [11], she had produced two healthy sons, in keeping with the family doctrine of the SS.

Lina had attended church regularly and was well aware of her husband's Catholic upbringing. He had even been an altar boy and although married in the Protestant faith, her husband had remained a Catholic. In 1935 however Lina became disillusioned with the Church and decided to leave, without telling her husband. In 1936, Heydrich confessed that he had forsaken the Church, feeling no longer able to practice his faith due to his politics, Heydrich considered the Church as a political power that presented a danger to the State and it would consequently be forever viewed in his eyes as one of the primary enemies, along with Freemasons, Jews and Marxists. Lina then admitted she had also abdicated her religion and left as a result of her beliefs. In the spring of that year, he declared his secession from the Church at the Berlin-Lichterfelde Lower Court [12].

Heydrich left the Church in Spring of 1936. Lina had left a year earlier.

Reichsführer-SS Heinrich Himmler would certainly have been pleased by the decision of the Heydrichs to leave the Church and would have undoubtedly been partly responsible for the decision. The SS was developing its own blend of Germanic religion, in which the Christian ethos had no place. In a speech made to his Gruppenführers in 1936, Himmler intimated that they should lead the way forward by leaving the Church. Many of the SS leadership corps left the Church that same year, others over subsequent years. Very few remained with the Church.

Gunter D'Alquen
Editor of the
'Das Schwarze Korps'

Possibly the Catholic Church had seen a threat coming from the new SS order since from 1934 they had forbidden priests to be members of the SS and even went to the lengths of excommunicating Geiste, a Catholic cleric in the SD. By 1937, the Church of Rome forbade it's priests to be members of the NSDAP. Heydrich's mother, still a fervent believer, fell out with her son over the arrest of the Bishop of Meissen [13].

1935 had seen the birth of the SS newspaper "Das Schwarze Korps", the first issue appearing on 6th March [14]. For the first time, the leadership of the SS was projected into the public eye. The twenty-four year old Gunter d'Alquen was appointed by Himmler, on Kurt Wittje's suggestion, to be the new editor. Heydrich was certainly the driving force behind this newspaper which was tolerated by Goebbels, probably because it claimed Hitler among

TIME OFF WITH THE FAMILY

The proud father with his son Klaus

Heydrich the family man. Although work kept him away from his family, when he was at home, Heydrich was the archetypal doting father and husband

Heydrich with his son Klaus

Heydrich with Klaus and Lina

Lina in a playful mood with their son Klaus. Her husband looks on. Such chances to have time off with thefamily became less and less as the Security Chief's workload increased.

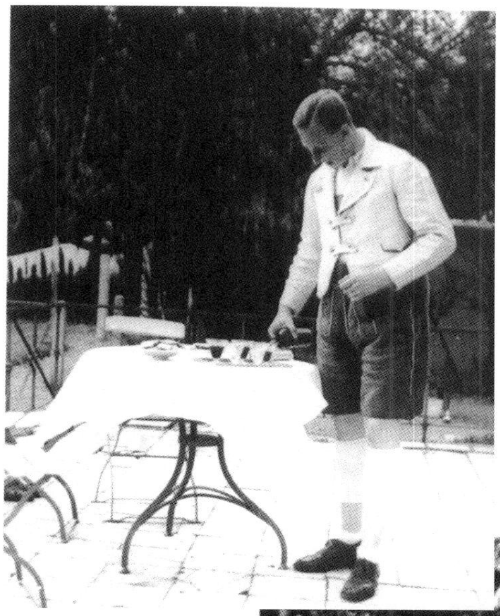

"Drinks for the guests"

Relaxing drinks at home with Lina and guests

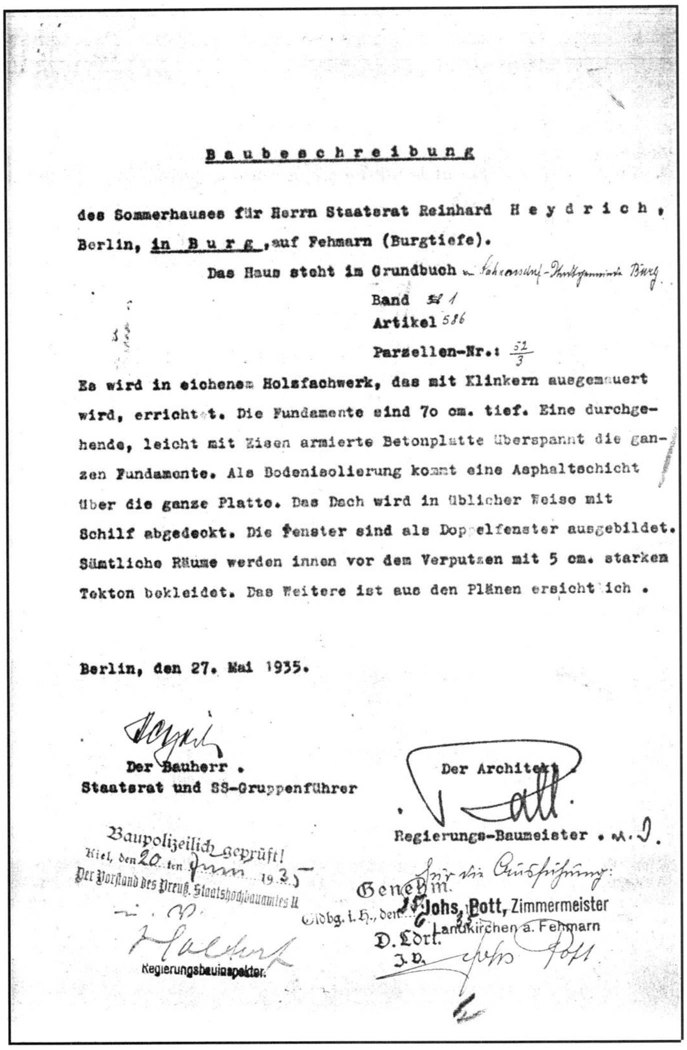

Baubeschreibung

des Sommerhauses für Herrn Staatsrat Reinhard Heydrich, Berlin, in Burg, auf Fehmarn (Burgtiefe).

Das Haus steht im Grundbuch

Band 1

Artikel 586

Parzellen-Nr.: 52/3

Es wird in eichenem Holzfachwerk, das mit Klinkern ausgemauert wird, errichtet. Die Fundamente sind 70 cm. tief. Eine durchgehende, leicht mit Eisen armierte Betonplatte überspannt die ganzen Fundamente. Als Bodenisolierung kommt eine Asphaltschicht über die ganze Platte. Das Dach wird in üblicher Weise mit Schilf abgedeckt. Die Fenster sind als Doppelfenster ausgebildet. Sämtliche Räume werden innen vor dem Verputzen mit 5 cm. starkem Tekton bekleidet. Das Weitere ist aus den Plänen ersichtlich.

Berlin, den 27. Mai 1935.

Der Bauherr.
Staatsrat und SS-Gruppenführer

Der Architekt.
Regierungs-Baumeister a. D.

Baupolizeilich geprüft!
Kiel, den 20. ten Juni 1935
Der Vorstand des Preuß. Staatshochbauamtes II
Regierungsbauinspektor.

Genehm.
Johs. Pott, Zimmermeister
Landkirchen a. Fehmarn

Gustav Rall
Heydrichs architect for the summer house

Left: This document dated 27th May 1935 details the construction materials for the summer house on Fehmarn. It is signed by Heydrich and his architect.

The Heydrichs' summer house built on Fehmarn. This photograph appeared as an advertisement after the war, when Lina and her daughter Marte were running the house as a Pension.

LIFE AS SECURITY CHIEF DID HAVE ITS FUNNY MOMENTS

After a pleasant afternoon spent in the company of Reichsführer-SS Himmler, his wife Marga and the Wolffs', a farewell is bid.............but trouble with the car !

Himmler offers a comical story and his wife Marga sniggers in the background nothing left for it, the car needs a push start !

This is a big car, everyone sees the funny side, the Reichsführer-SS the second most important man in Germany is needed to help push...Heydrich chuckles !

The women laugh and the men push, Lina Heydrich can be seen in the back seat, sitting next to Frieda Wolff, the wife of Karl Wolff.

Push harder giggle the women !

...and yes, the car fires up, the Heydrichs and Wolffs are at last on their way, out of the grounds of Himmler's home at Gmund.

.....AND SOME MOMENTS WERE FUNNIER THAN OTHERS !

Heydrich, Prinz Waldeck, von Eberstein, Lorenz and Rediess. A drink of wine and some theatrical conversation from von Eberstein.

Heydrich takes an 'occasional' cigarette, Prützmann is hidden behind Prinz Waldeck.

Prinz Waldeck tells a joke, Heydrich and the others listen. Rediess and Heydrich are already starting to laugh.

If only we knew what the joke was !...Heydrich cries with laughter.

The well known artist Wolfgang Willrich was asked by Heydrich to sketch a portrait of him. It was common place during this era to give portrait photographs, suitably dedicated, to friends and associates as gifts. Heydrich wished to give a portrait of himself as a present to Reichsführer-SS Himmler. The sketch was completed on the 13th December 1935 and given to Himmler as a Christmas (Julfest) present in that year. Contrary to popular opinion, Himmler and his Security Chief got on very well with each other. Interestingly this Willrich sketch was taken back to the USA in 1945 and survives in a collection to this day.

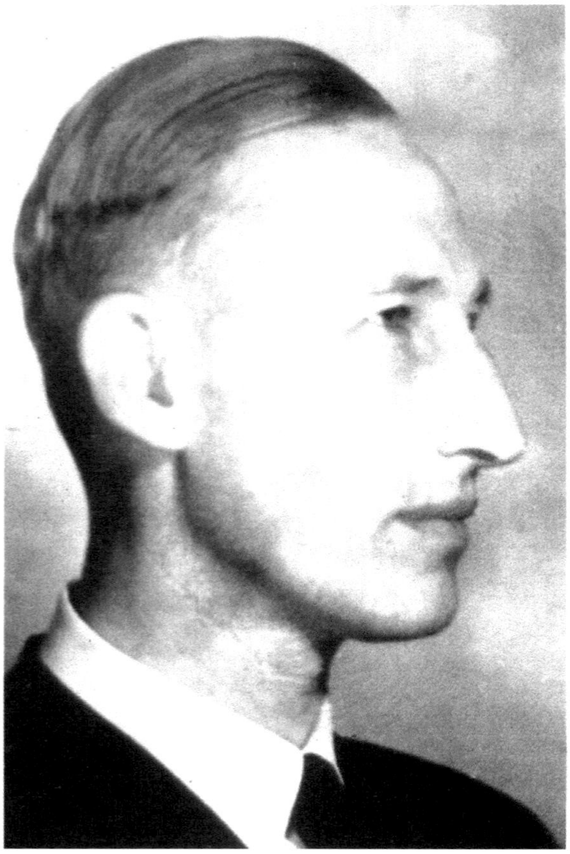

Two images of Heydrich, originally for use within identity books, it is interesting to note how well executed the drawing by Willrich is, in comparison to the above profile.

OFFICIAL ENGAGEMENTS

The position as Chief of the Security Service also meant being in the limelight. Heydrich is seen collecting money for the 'Winterhilfe', a charitable organisation to assist those in need.

Heydrich along with all of the SS leadership corps were expected to appear at the yearly 'Reichsparteitage' (National Rally Days) held at Nuremberg. Here he marches along with the other SS 'Hauptamtchefs' (Main Department Heads) saluting the 'Führer' Adolf Hitler at the 1935 Rally.

SS-Gruppenführer Heydrich with pensive look, photographed during one of the yearly rallies at Nuremberg.

During an official visit, Heydrich and other members of the SS leadership corps take a trip on a pleasure steamer. Here Heydrich talks to the crew. SS leaders Prützmann and Pancke can be seen behind him.

With Heydrich still talking to the crew of the steamer, Prützmann, Lorenz and Pancke can be seen behind him.

Occasionally Lina had the chance to accompany her husband on official engagements, such as this 'white shirt' engagement when Mussolini visited Germany in September 1937. Reinhard casts a loving look to his wife.

A 'snap shot' photograph of the Security Chief and his wife whilst taking an off duty stroll.

As well as the Nuremberg Rally Week, Heydrich would have been expected to attend other important events in the National Socialist calendar, such as the 9th November Commemorations in Munich and the yearly homage to Quedlinburg Cathedral to visit the grave of Heinrich I. Reichsführer-SS Himmler gives the salute, Wolff, Heydrich, Heissmeyer and Jeckeln can be seen behind him.

CHAPTER 8
CONSPIRACIES AT HOME AND ABROAD

Rudolf Formis was an electrical engineer, radio pioneer and former technical director of Radio Stuttgart, but was now working for a 'very different radio station', the Black Front organisation of Otto Strasser was operating from within the borders of Czechoslovakia and Formis was transmitting propaganda against the National Socialist regime.

On 9th January 1935, Heydrich summoned Alfred Naujocks, the SD 'Jack of all trades' to his office and advised him that the transmitter used by Formis had been located by direction finding devices and was situated about fifty or sixty kilometres south-west of Prague. He showed Naujocks a photograph of Formis and instructed him to bring the young man to Berlin, after destroying the transmitter [1].

Naujocks, obtained a false passport in the name of Gerber and, accompanied by a girlfriend of his fiancée, crossed into Czechoslovakia. He eventually discovered the transmitter to be in the Hotel Zahori in Dobris. 'Herr Gerber' and his 'wife' registered in the same hotel and obtained a wax impression of the key to Formis' room. He then returned to Berlin for instructions, leaving his partner at the hotel.

Heydrich re-iterated his earlier instructions and Naujocks as 'Herr Gerber' returned once again to Dobris, but this time he was accompanied by another agent, Gert Gröthe. On the night of 23rd January, the two undercover agents were about to surprise Formis and chloroform him when, to their surprise, Formis managed to pull a gun and a fight ensued. Naujocks was slightly wounded and Gröthe returned fire, hitting Formis in the head and killing him. The two agents were able to damage the transmitter before taking flight. Arriving in Heydrich's office on 24th January, they were treated to a dressing down from their Chief over their amateur methods.

This was not the only embarrassment that Heydrich suffered at the hands of his agents. A certain Berthold Jacob-Salomon had been writing well-informed articles on the secret re-armament of the Reichswehr in the left-wing publication 'World Stage'. Jacob-Salomon had left Germany early in 1933 to settle in Strasbourg, where he continued his articles with the Independent News Service; Heydrich was determined to silence him, but not before discovering his source.

In June 1934, the German Embassy in London reported that a German emigrant, by the name of Dr. Hans Wesemann, was willing to co-operate with the Gestapo. Wesemann was acquainted with Jacob-Salomon and therefore was ideal for tempting the unsuspecting dissident into the trap. Wesemann contacted Jacob-Salomon and they soon rekindled their relationship, with Wesemann supplying Jacob-Salomon with false Gestapo information for his news service. In October, Wesemann travelled to Strasbourg in order to build up confidence and encourage the belief in Jacob-Salomon's new found benefactor.

A kidnap attempt on Jacob-Salomon was decided, but the Gestapo was uneasy about the possibility of success in Strasbourg. Switzerland posed a much more tempting location so Basel was chosen, being only minutes from the Reich border. Wesemann informed Jacob-Salomon that an important and trusted friend would visit Basel, who desired a meeting, but was not happy to go to France where he might be compromised. The unsuspecting Jacob-Salomon agreed and duly arrived on 9th March at the Hotel St. Gotthard, as arranged, only to be directed to the restaurant Zum schiefen Eck, yards from the German frontier.

The three men met and enjoyed several drinks before, the collaborator of the group Manz, suggested they retire to his lodgings where they could fill out one of the blank passports that he carried. This would enable Jacob-Salomon to travel freely under an assumed name. Innocently, he agreed and a taxi was summoned, arriving immediately. The laughing trio climbed aboard and soon arrived at Adolf Hitler Strasse, just inside the Reich frontier. Jacob-Salomon was arrested by the Frontier Police and the two others returned to Switzerland.

The following day, in Berlin, Jacob-Salomon was interrogated by the Security Police Chief. Several suspected collaborators were arrested, but the startling truth was that Jacob-Salomon had obtained his information from the edition 'Reich Gazette' which published promotions and transfers. From this he had deduced the size and formations of different regiments and divisions, quite legally.

However, his future did not look promising in the clutches of the Gestapo. Wesemann had been arrested by

Alfred Naujocks, Heydrich's SD 'Jack of all Trades' was instructed by to destroy a transmitter being used to transmit propanganda against the National Socialist state and to bring the perpetrator, Formis back for interrogation. The mission went wrong and although the transmitter was disabled, Formis was accidently killed. Heydrich was not pleased.

Berthold Jacob-Salomon, a writer for a left-wing publication, kidnapped by Heydrich's SD. This resulted in an international incident. He was released on Hitler's orders in September 1935 and is photographed at a subsequent press conference.

the Swiss authorities who discovered what had happened, and in turn complained to the German Foreign Office and demanded Jacob-Salomon to be released. Initially, the Gestapo denied all knowledge of the abduction, it was only on the second demand that Hitler interceded and Jacob-Salomon was released in September 1935. Heydrich licked his wounds for the second time [2].

These ventures abroad were not the only sector of intelligence work that occupied Heydrich. He was spreading his wings further into the world of espionage. A conflict of interests soon emerged with the Reichswehr Counter-Intelligence Service, otherwise known as the 'Abwehr'. Naval Captain Conrad Patzig was chief of Military Counter-Intelligence and took an instant dislike to Heydrich, indeed the animosity appears to have been mutual. In late 1934, Patzig reported to, Admiral Canaris, that he could not tolerate Heydrich or his encroaching intelligence work any longer. The problem reached the ears of the minister responsible, Blomberg, and probably with the approval of Canaris, agreed to release Patzig from this position. Patzig's replacement was none other than Admiral Wilhelm Canaris himself, taking office on 2nd January 1935 [3].

Heydrich was delighted that his old navy friend would be a comrade in the field of intelligence, and because of their similar background, there was an immediate sense of co-operation between the two Chiefs. An agreement was reached between them on a future course of collaboration that would last until Heydrich's death. Lina insisted that her husband had no idea who Patzig's replacement was until a chance meeting one Sunday morning during a stroll near their rented house at Döllestrasse 31 in Berlin Südende. The Heydrichs came upon the Canaris family and the two men shook hands. Both were surprised to discover they were neighbours. It was the resumption of an old friendship, with the admiral's family regularly visiting the Heydrich household and playing croquet in their garden. Canaris reciprocated by inviting the SS family to his apartment at Döllestrasse 11 for meals. Lina states, *"My husband....was pleased that Canaris had taken over the job. They had both been in the Navy, after all, and that formed a bond between them"* [4].

When the Heydrichs later moved to a semi-detached house at Augustastrasse 14, in Berlin-Schlachtensee, they were surprised to discover that the Canaris family had also moved to the same district and that their garden adjoined the Heydrichs' hen house [4a]. Their social meetings were again resumed, with Reinhard and Erika Canaris once again resurrecting their musical talents. A string quartet regularly played at Augustastrasse 14 with the host taking first violin, Frau Canaris the second, Heinz Heydrich the cello and Ernst Hoffman, a friend of the Heydrich couple, the viola.

Canaris' biographer, Heinz Höhne, declares that Canaris approved of Heydrich and even looked upon him almost as a son. The often quoted theory that the two men hated each other and only remained in touch for professional reasons, does not appear to have any substance. The two friends continued to socialise until a few days before Heydrich's death.

There was, however, a certain amount of 'friendly' cunning and distrust on both parts. Canaris employed an Arab servant, Mohammed, who supposedly did not speak or understand German. He served the two intelligence chiefs at the Canaris house during private conversations. Heydrich expressed an uneasy feeling about his presence, but Canaris was quick to reassure his guest, reminding him of his lack of linguistic talent. One evening, Schmidt, the detective appointed to guard the Heydrich household, discovered Mohammed 'entertaining' a lady friend outside the Heydrich house, where he did not appear to have any problems speaking fluent German. Heydrich was convinced that Canaris was not to be trusted.

In late 1936, information reached the SD chief's ears that a high ranking Russian officer was planning to overthrow Stalin with the support of many officers. This was really the jurisdiction of the 'Abwehr' and Heydrich risked alienation from Canaris if he interfered, however not to miss out on a chance to damage the Soviet Army, he discussed the proposed overthrow with Himmler, and on Christmas Eve they reported the news to Hitler. Heydrich intended that the Russian officers should be unmasked, thereby unleashing Stalin's wrath upon the Russian Army General Staff. However, there was a flaw; the information eminated from a double agent in Paris, General Skoblin. He worked for both the SD and the Russian NKVD. The chief conspirator was identified as Marshal Mikhail Tukhachevsky. Hitler agreed to Heydrich's plan and authorised him to proceed.

During the following three months, Heydrich had Naujocks forge military documents with the signatures of Tukhachevsky. The SD's engraver, had little difficulty in reproducing correspondence between German officers and the unsuspecting Russian. There existed, in the German records, many documents with the signature and handwriting of Tukhachevsky from the post war period when the two armies collaborated. At the beginning of May 1936, SD Standartenführer Hermann Behrends delivered the documents to the

Heydrich and Canaris sit together with von Eberstein opposite, at a function held in Berlin during 1935. Various high ranking Generals of the army, navy and airforce are at the same table.

Marshal Tukhachevsky was planning to overthrow Stalin. Heydrich arranged for forged documents to be produced and surreptitiously put before Stalin's eyes. Tukhachevsky was immediately shot and a violent purge of the Russian officer corps began.

General Skoblin, a double agent. He worked for both the Russian NKVD and the German SD.

Admiral Wilhelm Canaris

Canaris took over command of Military Counter-Intelligence on 2nd January 1935. Heydrich was delighted that his old friend and naval companion was given this position. The friendship between Canaris and Heydrich would continue until Heydrich's death. Canaris was probably one of Heydrich's few true friends.

NKVD. He received three million roubles in exchange, which, for the most part, proved to be as genuine as the documents. Stalin received the file soon after. He already had suspicions regarding his high command, but this was 'proof positive'. How important a part Heydrich's connivance played in the scenario that followed, is still a matter for conjecture. On 12th June 1936, Tukhachevsky and several other senior Russian officers were shot. The killing did not end there, the executions heralded the start of the bloodiest political purge in the history of Stalin's Russia. Almost half the entire officer corps, some 35000, were eliminated; 90 per cent of all the generals, 80 per cent of the colonels, 3 out of 5 marshals, 13 out of 15 army commanders, 57 out of 85 corps commanders, 110 out of 195 divisional commanders and 220 out of 406 brigade commanders. All executed or cashiered. The Russian Army received a blow from within that took until the middle of the Second World War to recover; Heydrich was jubilant [5].

In May 1936, an assistant judge by the name of Ernst was examining a petty criminal, Otto Schmidt. He had previous convictions for theft, embezzlement and blackmail but on this occasion was arrested for blackmail plus a couple of minor offences. Ernst was obviously an accomplished interrogator, for he succeeded in gaining Schmidt's confidence. Incredibly the accused became the accuser and began talking openly about 'hundreds' of people he had blackmailed, including some prominent personalities whom he had allegedly captured participating in homosexual acts. He gave names.....SS Standartenführer Graf von Wedel, the Police President of Potsdam, Walther Funk, the Reichsminister for Economics, Rüdiger Graf von der Goltz and 'General' Fritsch. Ernst was startled. Which Fritsch could this be? Schmidt refused to say any more.

Josef Meisinger of the Gestapa Department for the 'Suppression of Homosexuality' was informed and Schmidt's case suddenly acquired importance. Were they now dealing with a case concerning the Commander-in-Chief of the Wehrmacht, Colonel-General Werner Freiherr von Fritsch? In July, Schmidt was confronted with a series of photographs, each displaying the subject's name, his attention was immediately drawn to the most impressive name and he identified the Colonel-General as "his" Fritsch.

Schmidt prepared and signed a statement which confirmed that he had been at the Berlin-Wannsee station in November 1933, when he saw a distinguished man dressed in a dark fur collared coat and monocle. This gentlemen left with an itinerant youth by the name of Martin Weingärtner. Schmidt followed them to an unlit area where he witnessed them perform a homosexual act, afterwards Schmidt followed the gentleman and confronted him, impersonating a police officer. The gentleman produced an identity card in the name of von Fritsch. An agreement was reached over a financial arrangement, but the gentleman had not sufficient cash on him, so they both went to Ferdinandstrasse 21 where the gentleman entered, shortly to return with part of the agreed sum. The balance was paid at a later date.

Meisinger realised the importance of this information since Von Fritsch was a well known opponent of the SS and was viewed by many in conservative circles as a leader of the opposition to Hitler. Meisinger reported to Heydrich, resulting in Himmler presenting the file to Hitler. Surprisingly, Hitler would not entertain any further action against the Army Chief and in fact ordered Himmler to destroy the file. Apparently he had no wish, at that particular time, to upset his army generals. Himmler complied, but not before Heydrich had the more important sections copied, in antisipation of their future use.

According to Colonel Fritz Hossbach, on 5th November 1937 Hitler held a conference with his senior service commanders: Göring of the Luftwaffe, Raeder of the Navy, von Fritsch of the Army, von Blomberg, his Minister of War and von Neurath, the Foreign Minister. He declared his intention to move east by 1943, if necessary by means of war. He remarked to Göring that he wished *"to put some steam up Fritsch's pants"*. Von Blomberg and von Fritsch both objected on military technicalities. Hossbach, Hitler's Wehrmacht adjutant, noted five days after the conference, *"At times the discussion became extremely heated, primarily during an argument between Blomberg and Fritsch on the one side and Göring on the other"* [6].

Hitler became disillusioned with his military advisers. Could this be the time to resurrect the Meisinger file on von Fritsch? Göring certainly thought so and duly instructed Meisinger to re-open it immediately. Inspector Fehlis, of the Gestapo, was tasked with the investigation and analysed the old evidence. On 15th January, 1938, Fehlis discovered that a retired Captain von Fritsch lived next door to Ferdinandstrasse 21, but did not investigate further [7]. Why the investigation was not pursued further isn't known but certainly many individuals would have been keen to see von Fritsch out of the way, including Heydrich and Himmler.

Meanwhile, another scandal was about to break. The Reichsminister for War, von Blomberg, was a widower with five children and after the death of his wife, he met and married a typist, Erna Gruhn, on 12th January 1938; Hitler and Göring were both witnesses. Shortly after, some obscene photographs were passed on to

Kurt Müller, head of the 'Reich Identification Office' of the 'RKPA'. His attention was drawn to a young woman who appeared naked in various indecent positions. The name of the subject had been written on the picture and it stuck in Müller's mind. Where had he seen that name before? He went to the files and discovered that the woman was none other than the Reichsminister's new wife [8].

Müller at once reported his findings to his chief, Arthur Nebe, who exclaimed, *"Good God Müller, this woman has kissed the Führer's hand!"* Nebe approached the Berlin Police President, Helldorf, who in turn went to General Keitel. He advised Helldorf to see Göring. Thus, on 23rd January, Göring obtained information that would lead to the downfall of his rival, Blomberg. Hitler received the news with a feeling of perplexity.

Göring now saw his chance of realising his ambition to become the Reichsminister for War. With Blomberg and Fritsch both out of the way, his route to the desired position was clear. Hitler directed that the Fritsch case be re-opened, but the wheels were already in motion. Fritsch received news of the impending bombshell with indignation totally denying the accusation and demanding an audience with Hitler, but at the Reich Chancellery he was confronted with Schmidt, who identified him as the gentleman in the coat with the fur collar and monocle.

Changes to the military hierarchy were made, however Göring had not anticipated Hitler's cunning. The Führer created a new High Command of the Armed Forces, with himself at the helm and the post of War Minister disappeared [9]. On 4th February, the press announced the changes. Von Blomberg and von Fritsch were retired; von Neurath was replaced by the faithful, but inept von Ribbentrop; sixteen generals were retired, forty-four received postings and the old War Ministry title was replaced by the new High Command of the Armed Forces (Oberkommando der Wehrmact).

The case against von Fritsch, however, was still outstanding. Hitler had intended that the Colonel-General should retire gracefully, but the proud army man had different ideas and insisted on having his chance to deny the accusation in public. Next, Hitler suggested a special court, but the military leaders, supported by the Reichsminister of Justice, Gürtner, sided with von Fritsch. Hitler reluctantly agreed to a Court Martial. The Gestapo was also ordered to conduct a corresponding investigation.

Von Fritsch's defenders then discovered the secret of Ferdinandstrasse. At Ferdinandstrasse 20 they discovered one Captain von Fritsch, who quickly admitted the Wannsee incident and informed them that the Gestapo had visited him as early as 15th January. The suppression of this crucial evidence by the Gestapo was now out in the open.

The army generals began to close ranks, the position of the Security Police, having started the case against von Fritsch as well as withholding evidence, became extremely precarious. Schellenberg relates that Heydrich became so nervous that, on one particular occasion, he summoned the former to his office and ordered him to bring a pistol. Nervously he said, *"If they don't start marching from Potsdam in the next hour and a half, the danger will have passed"* [10].

On 10th March, 1938, the court opened proceedings and delivered it's verdict on the following 18th March. Colonel-General von Fritsch was innocent on all counts [11]. Both Himmler and Heydrich were now in a very unstable position. Canaris and Hossbach formulated a list of demands for changes in the senior Gestapo officers which included the sacking of Himmler, Heydrich, Jost, Best, Meisinger and Fehlis. General Beck received the demands, but decided they should not be forwarded to Hitler. The Generals once again held back.

Hitler rehabilitated von Fritsch, but only to the post of Commander of the 12th Artillery Regiment. He was killed in action with this unit outside Warsaw on 22nd September, 1939 [12]. Himmler ordered the liar, Schmidt, to be shot and remained sensitive to the military for years to come. Heydrich had escaped the closest he had come to oblivion since his last brush with a military court in 1931.

Josef Meisinger headed the department for the suppression of homosexuality. He investigated the 'von Fritsch affair' and was later posted to Warsaw as SD Chief and subsequently transferred to Tokyo, for the duration of the war.

General Werner Freiherr von Fritsch accused of homosexuality by the SD. It later transpired that he was innocent and an army officer with the same name was the guilty party.

SD department chief, Arthur Nebe was told by Kurt Müller about von Blomberg's new wife. He exclaimed "Good God, Müller, this woman has kissed the Führer s hand !"

von Blomberg. It was found out that his second wife was a prostitute, Hitler promptly retired him from service.

Heydrich in conversation with General von Blomberg, the Reichs Minister for war, before the outbreak of the news about his new wife.

CHAPTER 9
AWAY FROM THE OFFICE

Heydrich was an extremely accomplished sportsman. As a memorandum from 16th December 1940 shows, he was nominated for the post as Inspector of Physical Training by Himmler [1] and for the 1936 Olympics, held a seat on the International Olympic Committee receiving all the privileges that went with it, much to the delight of his wife who obtained better stadium seating than Frau Himmler.

Lina Heydrich could not be described as a popular SS wife. She was considered rebellious by some since she often refused to fall in line with the wishes of her husband's chief, Reichsführer-SS Himmler. At one point, Frieda Wolff, the wife of SS General Karl Wolff was tasked with the unenviable job of counselling Lina and advising her of Himmler's misgivings. On a visit to the sailing regatta in Kiel, Frau Wolff informed Lina that Himmler was not happy with her behaviour, in particular her failure to show respect to the Reichsführer and his wife, furthermore she did not always comply with orders. Understandably, Lina believed that her private life was her own and refused to give up any freedom that was imposed by her position as an SS leaders wife.

It was realised by Lina quite quickly that this counselling session had hidden implications. Karl Wolff was keen to replace Reinhard Heydrich as Security Chief and this interview was a test, not of Lina, but of Reinhard [2]. History shows that Wolff was unsuccessful in his ambitions, even failing to replace Heydrich after his death, but by then he probably had no wish to be involved with the thankless task of RSHA Chief. Lina continued to be her own woman.

Augustastrasse 14, the new home for the Heydrichs' situated in the Berlin suburb of Schlachtensee. Photograph taken in 1997.

At the end of February 1937, the Heydrich family moved from Döllestrasse into a large house on a new estate at Augustastrasse 14, Berlin-Schlachtensee. The house consisted of four bedrooms for the family, two reception rooms, a dining room, kitchen and cellar. On the top floor there was a room for the servants. Reinhard had employed a second domestic. The garden had an open terrace where Lina built a chicken coup, she also erected a tall hedgerow around the property and planted fruit trees in her 'protest garden'. The house cost them 49000 Reichmarks and sat in a plot measuring 700 square metres. They were more than satisfied with their position.

On the morning of his 33rd birthday on the 7th March, Lina surprised her husband with a piano from the recently dissolved Halle conservatory. Reinhard declared that they should take the honeymoon he still owed her and produced two tickets for a Mediterranean trip, Lina was overjoyed.

Lina worried about their lack of friends, since her husband shunned the possibility of becoming too familiar with acquaintances, believing that he could not afford the position in which too many close relationships might place him. He once asked Himmler not to refer to him with the familiar German term "Du", strongly believing that he would be unable to argue against some of Himmler's plans if they were considered as such close friends. Heydrich's logical protestations against his Reichsführer's more fantastic ideas often resulted in Himmler's retort, *"Oh, Heydrich, you with your damned logic!"* [3].

With the imposed restriction on establishing close friendships, Lina became increasingly lonely and the couple discussed their situation. Reinhard took his wife's head in his hands and said, *"Do we need friends? You are my best friend. We don't need to share it with anyone. Let's carry on the way it is"* [4]. Lina related in her autobiography, that she realised at that moment how her life was tied to the thoughts, wishes and dreams of her husband.

Every morning, the SS-Gruppenführer rose early to wait for his barber to arrive and shave him. He took breakfast with his wife and left for the office, arriving no later than eight. Heydrich's routine included the weekends, staying at his desk until noon.

Berlin Olympics 1936

Heydrich sat on the International Olympic Committee and was nominated by Reichsführer-SS Himmler as Inspector of Physical Training. In this photograph from the 1936 Olympics, Heydrich can be seen in a light coloured suit standing centre left behind Hitler.

Soon after arriving at his office, he would attend the gymnasium for a period of fencing with his instructor, Dr. Hoops. Heydrich fenced with the foil and sabre, Lina states that this was primarily to relieve the stress of his working life, rather than for competition.

With the expansion of his responsibilities, a four seater aeroplane was made available for Heydrich's use. His pilot was Hauptmann Leopold and between them, they hatched a plan to secretly teach Heydrich to fly. Lina soon discovered why her husband was getting up one hour earlier in the morning; in order to practice his aerobatics. Heydrich acquired a bi-plane and soon became proficient at rolls, spins, loops and flying upside down!

Enthusiastic for his new found sport, Heydrich gained the use of a field near their home on Fehmarn and erected a chalet. This would enable him to visit the family at weekends by aeroplane when they were on the island. He signalled his arrival to Lina below by flying over their house and gunning the engine. She would then prepare his food, a local dish of fried potatoes and 'Krum and milk'. The 'dreaded' head of the Gestapo would often be seen pedalling his way to and from his house to the airfield on an old bicycle.

On one occasion, Heydrich suggested that his wife might wish to accompany him in his plane. She examined his pilot's licence before agreeing! As they climbed above the island, he pointed out the village of Albertsdorf getting smaller and smaller. Once back on 'terra firma', Lina expressed no further desire to fly.

As her husband's aeronautical skills improved, he progressed to flying fighters at Staaken airfield near Berlin, and subsequently during the war, saw active duty with the Luftwaffe. Heydrich achieved all this despite an order from Himmler, dated 27th May 1937, that both he and SS-Obergruppenführer Fritz Weitzel were forbidden to pilot their own aeroplanes [5]. Apparently, the Reichsführer-SS was concerned about their lack of experienced flying time after an adjutant of the Führer, was fatally injured piloting an aircraft.

The duties of SS-Gruppenführer and Chief of Security increasingly took Heydrich away from his family to the point that their marriage was put under pressure. Everything to do with home life fell on Lina's shoulders, after complaining to her husband, he agreed to spend more time at home, but soon returned to his previous behaviour. At one stage Lina considered leaving her husband, however, salvation was at hand in the form of Walter Schellenberg, a young assessor in Heydrich's office.

Walter Schellenberg

Schellenberg had recently married, but was having problems with his wife so he approached Frau Heydrich for help. She agreed to invite Frau Schellenberg to the Heydrichs' hunting lodge at Parlow. There they talked and she discovered that Schellenberg's wife was jealous of her young and handsome husband. Suddenly, Lina realised that jealousy could possibly help the relationship with her own husband. Dangerously, she decided to invite Schellenberg to visit more often and as anticipated they became close friends.

Heydrich soon noticed the attention being paid to his wife by the young Schellenberg. In Schellenberg's memoirs, (whose authenticity is now viewed with some doubt), he describes an incident that resulted from Heydrich's suspicions. Schellenberg was invited to a bar by Heydrich and Gestapo Chief Heinrich Müller where he was given a drink. Suddenly, the atmosphere changed and Heydrich is alleged to have informed Schellenberg that his drink had been laced with a poison (the only known antidote being in a file in Heydrich's pocket). Unless Schellenberg admitted everything that had occurred between him and Frau Heydrich, he would be left to die. If he were honest and forthright, he would be given the antidote. Schellenberg insisted that nothing had happened between him and the lady in question, other than conversation. According to Schellenberg, whether his boss believed him or not, he was given another drink containing the antidote.

This story does seem a little far fetched and, bearing in mind the doubts now cast on the validity of the Schellenberg memoirs, one must judge for oneself if there is any truth in this anecdote. However, it does smack of the 'Boys Own' type of spy yarn that was so popular with the younger Heydrich and would undoubtably appeal to his sense of humour.

With the expansion of his responsibilities, a four seater aeroplane was placed at Heydrich's disposal. Heydrich was excited by the idea of flying and managed to persuade his pilot Captain Leopold to teach him. It wasn't long before he had purchased a bi-plane and was practising aerobatics.

Aktbeleg: 12 Schriftgutverwaltung 2

Aktennotiz: Heydrich G.

Ich habe heute in Gegenwart des ϟϟ-Gruppenführers W o l f f ~~dem~~ ϟϟ-Obergruppenführer W e i t z e l und ϟϟ-Gruppenführer H e y d r i c h verboten, während ihrer aktiven Dienstzeit als ϟϟ-Obergruppenführer bzw. ϟϟ-Gruppenführer ein Flugzeug selbst zu steuern.

Anlass zu diesem Verbot hat mir der tödliche Absturz des Adjutanten des Führers, Hauptmann Manzius, gegeben.

Fliegen erfordert ständige Übung, die jedoch nicht vorhanden ist, wenn nur nach längeren Pausen geflogen wird. Dies ist bei ϟϟ-Obergruppenführer Weitzel und ϟϟ-Gruppenführer Heydrich der Fall, da ihnen ihr Dienst keine Zeit für ständiges Fliegen lässt.

Der Reichsführer-ϟϟ

Berlin, den 27. Mai 1937.

An die
<u>ϟϟ-Personalkanzlei</u>
zur Beinahme zum Personalakt des ϟϟ-Obergruppenführers Weitzel und ϟϟ-Gruppenführers Heydrich übersandt.

Following a fatal accident involving one of Hitler's adjutants, Reichsführer-SS Himmler forbade both Heydrich and another SS General, Fritz Weitzel from piloting their own planes. The above document dated 27th May1937 states that the two SS leaders are from this day forbidden from piloting their own planes. Heydrich ignored the order. It was only much later during the war when Heydrich's plane came down over enemy lines,a situation that came to the attention of Hitler, that his independant flying days were over.

Whenever the opportunity arose, Heydrich became involved in sporting pursuits. He had long been a competent sailor, learning much of his sailing skills during his time as a naval cadet. Here the Security Chief shows how to set the sails.

SUMMER DAYS ON FEHMARN

The Heydrichs' summer house on the Isle of Fehmarn was conveniently situated next to the beach. Above: Heydrich with Klaus by the sea, laughing, presumably because Klaus doesn't want to go in the water. Below: Lina, Reinhard and their two boys, Klaus and Heider.

"Love Match"
Lina and Reinhard enjoy a summer game of tennis.

Lina playfully teases one of their boys, Reinhard smiles.

WINTER SPORTS IN AUSTRIA

Heydrich always enjoyed the winter sports season. Here at Kitzbühl, he watches the ski-ing with Daluege, Frick and Gauleiter Hofer.

Heydrich chats and has a joke with the SS ski-ing team.

Heydrich and Daluege check the competition papers, although their relationship had an awkward start, they became quite friendly.

Above: Heydrich and Daluege, photographed at the same event as the one on the proceeding page. Below: Heydrich and Daluege in conversation with one of the SS ski-ing team.

Back again to Kitzbühl in 1941, Heydrich in conversation with the Kreisleiter of Kitzbühl

Lina's initial objective was however successful, her Reinhard spent more time with his family. The Schellenberg marriage, however, did not fair so well, coming to an end with Frau Schellenberg throwing acid into her husband's face [6].

On 9th April 1939, a baby girl, Silke, was born to the reconciled couple [7]. Heydrich had only ever wanted boys and Lina was worried that he would not favour a daughter. Her fears were totally unfounded, the proud father showing off his baby daughter to everyone. They became inseparable and Reinhard displayed more than ever that he was a loving, father and husband.

During this time Lina advised her husband to cultivate a certain level of social contact with his subordinates, he agreed and Lina took responsibility for looking after the wives. Lina organised a sports club for the women, while her husband provided a suitable hall and a qualified trainer, Hartnagel. At first, the wives were reluctant, but felt obliged to join in. Hartnagel certainly had his work cut out, trying to loosen up the stiff and embarrassed women, but eventually he succeeded.The club was a great success, with eight 'Gestapo ladies' winning their gold sports badges and twenty their silver.

One of the women, an ex-dancer volunteered to teach them to dance. Suitable women were chosen, including Lina. The wives, fiancées and girlfriends of the Gestapo and SD invited their men to a social evening at the Berlin Kroll Opera. Lina organised a traditional folk group of around fifteen or twenty girls from Fehmarn, they sang old German folk songs and danced. Later appearing as revue girls, they wore froufrou (dancing dresses), black stockings along with high patent leather boots and danced the can can. At last Lina was enjoying a normal social life that she had missed for quite a while.

Lina also accompanied her husband when he went horse riding. They often rode with Doctor Ferdinand Sauerbruch, Lilli and Max de Crinis. Walter Schellenberg also joined them on occasions at the stables of the retired cavalry officer, Captain Rose, in Berlin. Heydrich and Schellenberg were the only accomplished riders of the group and would often gallop off together. Afterwards, the group would retire to the de Crinis house at Wannsee for champagne breakfasts, these were still the peaceful pre-war times (by the War's end, Lilli and SS-Standartenführer Professor Doctor Max de Crinis were to take their own lives) [8].

Soon after the Austrian Anschluss in 1938, Frau Elisabeth Kaltenbrunner invited Lina to visit her in Linz. Lina took to her at once. She was introduced to Elisabeth's parents and immediately felt at home. The two women travelled to Vienna together where their husbands were in separate hotels. Lina describes Ernst Kaltenbrunner as dynamic, rough and uncouth. *"His hands were paws, large and broad, his face displayed rough pores. When I leave, Ernst Kaltenbrunner takes me to the station. He finds my sleeping compartment and tries to hug me farewell. I avoid him and accidentally bump into another passenger. It is Hans Moser, the actor. He mumbles and feels his way along the corridor.....he is drunk"* [9].

Lina did not harbour any fond memories of her husband's successor. The Kaltenbrunners only visited once more, this time at the Heydrich house in Berlin. However the old immediate friendship with Elisabeth was no longer there, having been replaced with an air of mistrust. They did not meet again.

Both Lina and her husband enjoyed the company of the Backes'. Herbert Backe was the State Secretary in Darré's Ministry of Agriculture and later replaced his boss as Minister, with the SS rank of Obergruppenführer [12]. He became a very close friend with the security Chief, the two men had very similar ideas and both held great respect for each other. The families often socialised, even their respective children got on well with each other. Post-war Lina spoke very highly of Backe, praising his efforts to keep the people alive when food was running out. Unfortunately Herbert Backe was one of many to commit suicide at the end of the war.

Before the war, Heydrich, in his capacity as Secretary of State reported to Himmler and as such, had no direct access to Hitler. Only at official functions at the Reich Chancellery or the Führerbau in Munich would Heydrich have the opportunity to discuss matters with Hitler, one to one. Lina remembers an occasion when she attended a function with her husband and met Hitler, it was at the Reich Chancellery *"Hitler stood in the vestibule. We approach him. He stretches out both hands and says spontaneously, 'What a lovely couple, I am most impressed'. Reinhard grins"* [10].

That same evening, Lina also met the Todt couple. She remembered Fritz Todt as an extremely intelligent man with the ability to hold a lively conversation. *"Reinhard also held him in great esteem"*, Lina later stated. His successor, Albert Speer, did not receive the same accolade. Heydrich considered Speers' appointment

Above: The Heydrich family.The two boys, Klaus and Heider look at their sister Silke. Below left: A photograph from 1941 showing Heydrich with his daughter Silke, contrary to worries by Lina, Reinhard adored his daughter. Below: Notice placed in the 'Das Schwarze Korps' by the Heydrichs for the birth of their daughter.

ᛉ
Silke
9. April 1939

Die Geburt unseres dritten Kindes, eines Sonntagsmädels, zeigen in dankbarer Freude an

Lina Heydrich, geb. von Osten
Reinhard Heydrich
SS-Gruppenführer und
Chef der Sicherheitspolizei

Berlin-Schlachtensee

After difficulties with their marriage (brought on by the amount of time the Security Chief was away from home), the ever faithful Reinhard promised Lina to spend more time with the family. The reconciled Heydrichs' had a third child on the 9th April 1939.

Three of the most powerful members of Reichsführer-SS Himmler's leadership corps, from left to right Heydrich head of Security, Pohl head of Administration and Wolff Chief Adjutant to the Reichsführer.

Before the war, Heydrich had no direct access to Hitler. Any communication went via Heydrich's immediate superior Reichsführer-SS Himmler. Occasionally at official functions or when invited to the Berghof, Heydrich would have the possibility to talk directly to Hitler. Photograph taken at the Berghof where Himmler, Heydrich and Wolff are in conversation.

SS General and State Secretary for Food & Agriculture Herbert Backe

Backe was one of Heydrich's close friends, both families would socialise together.

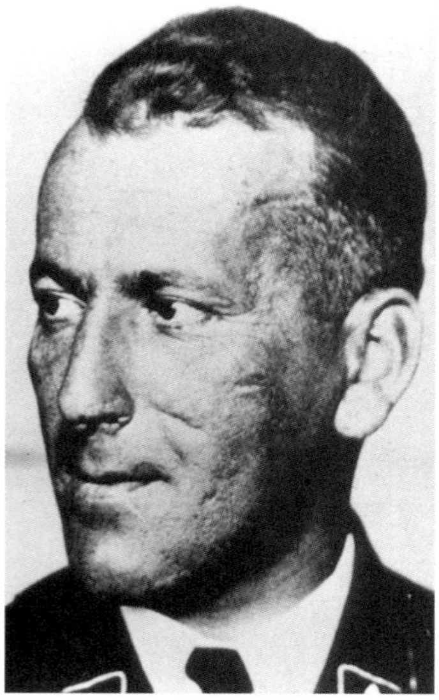

Ernst Kaltenbrunner

He was not particualy liked by Lina.

Fritz Todt

Lina remembered Todt as an intelligent and interesting man to talk to. Her husband also held him in high esteeem.

Secretary of State Paul Körner

Heydrich blamed Körner for the loss of their hunting lodge near Schorfheide, perhaps n part to calm Lina down over her rage with Reichsmarschall Göring.

Reichsmarschall Hermann Göring

He wished to extend his hunting grounds which included a parcel of land leased by the Heydrichs'. Lina was furious.

Reinhard and Lina leased a section of land at Parlow, outside Berlin, as they both enjoyed tracking and hunting. Heydrich, Daluege and Reichsführer-SS Himmler pose for this photograph during a hunt.

as a major mistake by Hitler. Lina points out that her husband and Speer had little personal contact. Speer visited them in Prague and was escorted around the city by his host, but this was only a rare visit. Lina criticises one of Speer's books in which he describes Himmler. It is interesting to note what Lina and her husband's thoughts were of the SS Chief:

Commenting post-war, Lina states *"I only read Speer's book as I hoped to find enlightenment regarding Himmler from an upper echelon viewpoint. I find it inexplicable how Himmler seems to have slipped Speer's memory. For us, Himmler was always our heaviest and biggest problem. In contrast to Speer's opinion, I found Himmler as especially intelligent and unbelievably well read, one who wished to translate that which he read into reality, and in that, did not see reality soberly enough. Hence the scurrilous goings on. We laughed more about his hobbies than feared them. Only it cost us much effort to talk him out of them again. We walked to the Externstein, viewed the Irminsul from all angles and also heard without emotion his theories over pagan stones, hero groves and similar. That did not harm anyone. Quite the contrary, it frequently provoked thought; but we did not see him as a good 'post filler'. In our opinion, Himmler was, and we knew him very well, the wrong man for the post in which Hitler had placed him. He was neither soldier nor politician, neither sportsman nor organiser. He was a despised intellectual and nobody knew that better than those who had to work for him. He, who gave us many useful as well as useless ideas.......was never the real or actual leader of the SS. The SS carried him, protected him and supported him. They made the best of what he had to offer. The leading people like Reinhard were never his blind followers. They never allowed control to be taken out of their hands. He was not even in the position of being able to give plausible explanations for things that occurred within his sphere of competence, even when people, because of their position, knew what was going on. So he answered my question, as to what took place in the concentration camps, with the answer that they had been mainly converted to armaments production"* [11].

In August 1938, at the age of 75, Bruno Heydrich died. His funeral took place in Halle at the Magdalenenkapelle der Moritzburg, followed by the internment at the Stadtgottesäcker. The funeral was attended by many high ranking SS officers, and wreaths along with messages of sympathy were sent by important Party officials including Hermann Göring and Heinrich Himmler [13]. Had it not been previously apparent, it was now obvious that the young Heydrich was being groomed for greater things. Could he be the next Reichsführer-SS in waiting?

The Heydrichs leased a piece of land at Parlow, adjacent to the forest Schorfheide, outside Berlin and developed it into a hunting area and employed a gamekeeper, Adolf Koeppen, a carpenter by trade. High seats were erected along with hides and paths, there was also a hunting lodge. Lina enjoyed this land and became proficient at tracking and hunting. Hermann Göring had erected a large hunting lodge on the Schorfheide, which he called "Karinhall" after his first wife. Göring decided that he would extend his land and this included the area around Parlow. The Heydrichs were appalled to discover that they had to give up their lease. Lina was all for fighting Göring over the matter, but interestingly and perhaps prudently her husband was less keen to engage in a fight with Hitler's old friend. Consequently, Heydrich's adjutant, Police Major Pomme, himself a keen hunter, found an alternative lease for the Heydrichs at Stolpshof and much to the disgust of Lina, they moved.

On their first visit to their new land at Stopshof, Lina expressed her feelings, calling Göring *"....scoundrel, the pot belly, that overfed piece of humanity can't grab enough.......he is nothing more than a trigger happy dog"* [14]. Reinhard was at first silent before quietly saying, *"That is not Göring, perhaps he knows nothing of this. This is definitely the work of his Secretary of State, Körner"* [15].

The new estate consisted of twenty hectares. Under a National Socialist law, anyone who was not a farmer was forbidden to own or lease any land in excess of seven hectares. Lina took a farming apprenticeship and studied agriculture at the Chamber of Agriculture in Brandenberg, passing her examinations. In later years after the death of her husband she would put this experience to good use in Bohemia Moravia.

Christmas 1941 was the last time the couple hunted at Stolpshof. Lina Heydrich mentioned in her post-war autobiography that they went on a midnight stalk. They would soon all be moving to Prague where Reinhard had already been for three months.

Reinhard Heydrich's father Bruno died in August 1938. He had been unwell for some time.

Bruno Heydrich's coffin is carried to the Stadtgottesacher in Halle. It would seem that the grave no longer exists.

Nach langem Leiden hat mein lieber guter Mann, unser guter Vater und Großvater

Konservatoriums-Direktor

Richard Bruno Heydrich

im Alter von 76 Jahren seine Augen für immer geschlossen.

Frau Elisabeth Heydrich, geb. Krantz
Reinhard Heydrich, SS-Gruppenführer und Chef der Sicherheitspolizei
Heinz Heydrich, SS-Obersturmführer und Schriftleiter
Frau Maria Heindorf, geb. Heydrich
Frau Lina Heydrich, geb. von Osten
Frau Trude Heydrich, geb. Werther
Wolfgang Heindorf, Abteilungsleiter im Zentralbüro DAF.
und 7 Enkelkinder.

Die Beisetzung erfolgte am Sonnabend, dem 27. August 1938, auf dem Stadtgottesacker in Halle a. d. S.

Left. mention of the funeral of Bruno Heydrich was placed in the SS magazine 'Das Schwarze Korps'. Both Lina and Reinhard Heydrich attended the funeral along with other family members such as Reinhard's sister Maria and brother Heinz who was an Obersturmführer in the SS.

Below:A large number of SS high leaders came to the funeral out of respect for the Security Chief.

Abschied von Bruno Heydrich

Die Beisetzung auf dem Stadtgottesacker. (Aufnahme: Daaz)

Die Trauer- und Abschiedsfeier für den verstor- | klang die Feierstunde aus mit dem „Vater unser

CHAPTER 10
THE FENCER

Whatever drove Heydrich in his official capacity as head of the vast network of police departments, it permeated through to his love of sport. He possessed a determination beyond comparison within the ranks of the black order to succeed in competition. His love of horse riding, athletics, skiing, swimming, sailing and shooting was only surpassed by his enthusiasm for flying and fencing.

Dr.Hoops
Heydrich's fencing trainer

Fencing appears to have been his most successful pastime in the sporting arena and was, by his own admission, his passion. Even in later years, he would always spend time to exercise his skills with Dr. Hoops before starting his strenuous days at the office. His efforts paid off. At the order of the Reichsführer-SS, the first SS Fencing Masters Tournament was held in the Berlin House of German Sport from 12th to 14th November 1936. The SD was heavily represented. Heydrich was placed fifth in the rapier class A and third in the sabre class A. SD men won both class A competitions in the foil and rapier and also attained second place in the sabre class A. During the evening of the 14th, in the officers' mess at the Lichterfelde barracks of the SS Leibstandarte Adolf Hitler, SS-Obergruppenführer Heissmeyer presented the prizes. Heydrich gave a speech emphasising the importance of fencing in the SS culture [1]. In August 1941, at the second wartime German fencing championships in Bad Kreuznach, Heydrich was placed fifth out of the top twelve fencers in the country [2].

Following his death, a top German sports official, Herbert E. von Daniels, wrote a commemorative article in the newspaper 'Physical Training and Education'. He describes Heydrich as follows: *"Those who know him are aware that he will not relax.......His base attitude towards sport, as much as towards work, is one of incessant activity, always pushing himself and striving to improve.........One only really got to know comrade Heydrich on the days following such successes. However pleased he himself might be about his victories, he didn't make much fuss about them. Now and then he would encourage his comrades with a joke if they had not been as successful as himself. The hours spent training with him or in his company after the bouts were unforgettable"* [3].

Deschner describes how, in December 1941, when the war for Heydrich was at it's peak, he stepped in to fill a last minute vacancy in the German national team who were playing against the superior Hungarians. Although he had no opportunity to prepare and train with the other members of the team, Heydrich gained top position amongst his compatriots and second best overall in the sabre fencing. This prompted a sports journalist to comment, *"...an almost unimaginable result when one considers the amount of other work he still managed"* [4].

However, not everyone had the same view towards the chief of the 'Reichssicherheitshauptampt' (Reich Security Head office). Some were relieved when he left the arena without causing any ill feeling. His attitude had been shown as unsportsmanlike on occasions, particually when disputing decisions of the judges. Bruno Streckenbach stated that he often heard the comment, *"He can never lose, only complain"* [5]. Heydrich was aware of his shortcomings, requesting Dr. Hoops to quickly point out to him when his behaviour was becoming unsuitable. His position as head of the feared Gestapo did not always impress his opponents. One referee in particular publicly reprimanded him for questioning a decision. Heydrich was astounded, but reluctantly accepted the admonishment.

Fellow SS fencers idolised their leading swordsman, which was not surprising since their successful Gruppenführer always offered them encouragement. At the earliest opportunity Heydrich would do his utmost to help young up and coming fencers, and indeed would always try to entice those showing exceptional talent, to join the ranks of the SS. If they were not so keen to join voluntarily, attempts would be made to have them assigned to the SS. Heydrich would stop at nothing to attain the best team for the SS and promoted the idea that good fencers would be far better off within that organisation.

Heydrich even contravened official NSDAP policy if it interfered with his fencing. At the request of his SS fencers, he assisted Paul Sommer, a former German champion and a Jew under the Nuremberg Laws, to

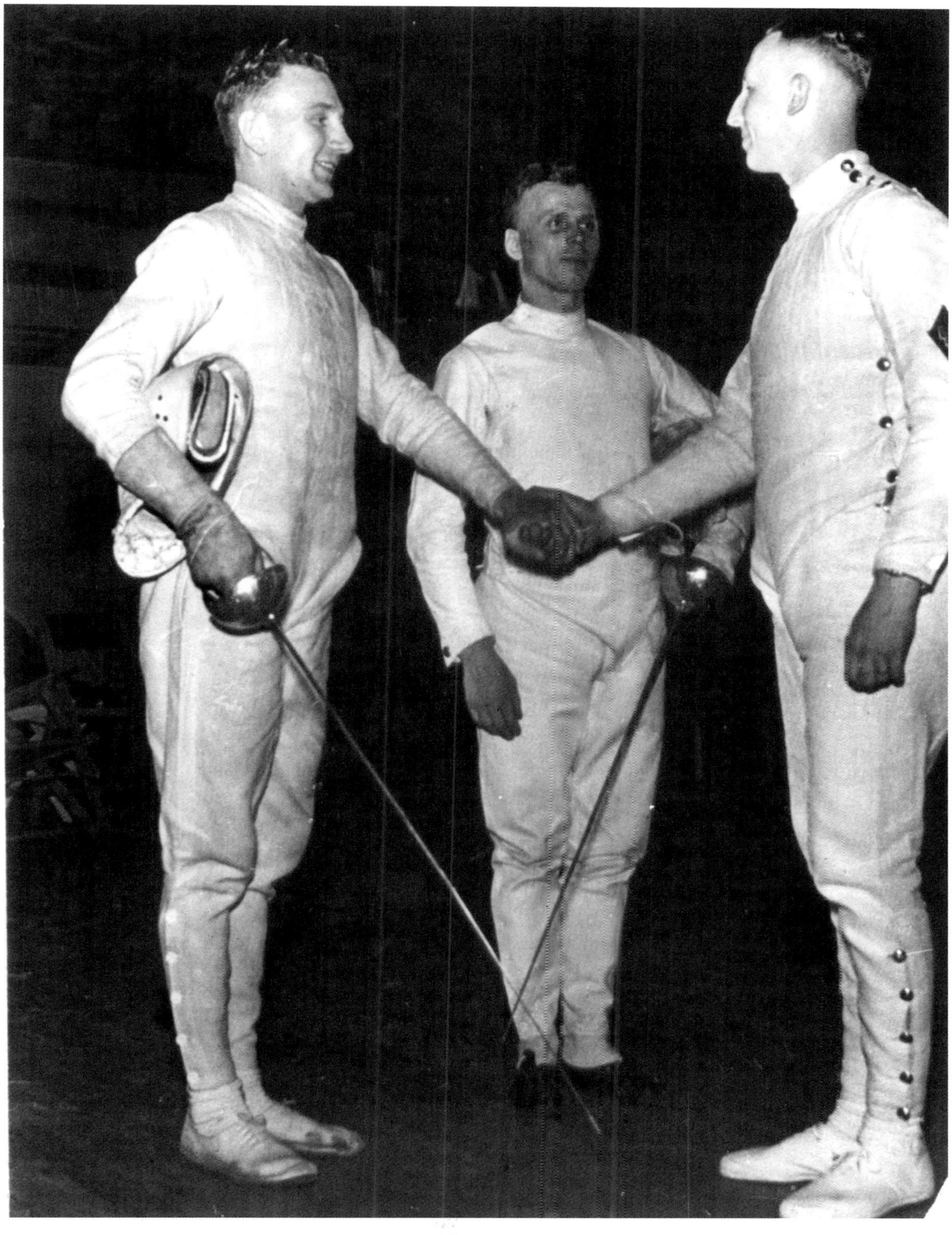

Heydrich offers his congratulations to SS-Untersturmführer Kretschmann at the 1936 SS fencing championships

Heydrich was without doubt one of the top fencers in the country at that time. Although hugely competitive and often victorious, he was never boastful about his successes. He was greatly admired by his fellow team members who he encouraged. His comments about the importance of fencing within the SS culture would have fallen in exactly with Himmlers' beliefs since both saw the SS in terms of a 'greater family'.

Heydrich in action on the left.

A content looking Heydrich stands with his winning team and their trophy.

Heydrich receives a citation and award after winning a fencing competition.

The SS fencing team pose for the camera. At the rear stands their trainer Dr.Hoops. He was nominated as a liaison officer with the International Fencing Federation (F.I.E.)

Heydrich with his fencing team.

Der Reichsführer SS
Der Chef des Sicherheitshauptamtes

Berlin SW 11, den 2. November 1936
Prinz Albrechtstr. 8,
Zimmer 104.

Herrn

E h l i n g

<u>in B e r l i n .</u>

Sehr geehrter Herr E h l i n g !

In der Zeit vom 11. bis 14. November dieses Jahres finden in Berlin die ersten SS-Meisterschaften im Fechten statt. SS-Gruppenführer Heydrich, der Sie aus Ihrer Tätigkeit als Kampfrichter auf den olympischen Spielen und anderen Gross-Turnieren her kennt, hat mich beauftragt, Sie zu bitten, sich für die Zeit der Meisterschaften als Kampfrichter zur Verfügung zu stellen.

Es ist selbstverständlich, dass Sie während dieser Zeit vollkommen Gast der SS sind und Ihnen keine Ausgaben für Unterkunft, Verpflegung und Fahrgelder entstehen werden. Ich bitte Sie daher, mir umgehend, jedoch bis spätestens Donnerstag, den 5. November, Ihren Bescheid zukommen zu lassen, ob wir auf Ihre liebenswürdige Unterstützung rechnen dürfen.

Anreisetag: Mittwoch, den 11. November 1936
Florett: Donnerstag, den 12. November 1936 }
Degen: Freitag, den 13. November 1936 } pünktlich
Säbel: Sonnabend, den 14. November 1936 } morgens 8h
Siegerehrung: Sonnabend, den 14. November 1936 abends 20h
Kasino der Leibstandarte SS-Adolf-Hitler
Gemeinsamer Ausflug: Sonntag, den 15. November 1936.

Heil Hitler!

Dr. Hoops

SS-Untersturmführer

Br.

Heydrich's personal fencing trainer Dr.Hoops was asked to help with the organisation of the first SS fencing championships, which were to be held in Berlin from the 11th to 14th November 1936. In this letter dated 2nd November, Dr.Hoops asks Herr Ehling, who had acted as the referee at the Olympic Games and other major competitions, if he would referee at the SS chamionships. Dr.Hoops added that SS-Gruppenführer Heydrich had commissioned Hoops to invite Ehling as the referee and that Ehling would come as a guest of the SS, therefore all his expences would be paid. An answer was recuired by the 5th November and a timetable laid out detailing the various disciplines.

Der Reichsführer SS
Der Chef des Sicherheitshauptamtes

Der Fechtsportreferent

Berlin SW 11, den 9. November 1936
Prinz Albrecht-Str. 8
Zimmer 104

Herrn

E h l i n g,

in Berlin NW 7

Friedrichstr. 122/123

Sehr geehrter Herr E h l i n g!

SS-Gruppenführer H e y d r i c h hat mich beauftragt, Ihnen für die freundliche Zusage, die SS-Meisterschaften im Fechten als Kampfrichter zu unterstützen, seinen Dank auszusprechen.

Ich bitte Sie, am Mittwoch, den 11. November, abends 20 1/2 Uhr im Gastzimmer des Hotels Rheinland - Koch-, Ecke Wilhelmstraße - zu erscheinen. Dort werden Sie Ihre Kampfrichterausweise erhalten.

Heil Hitler!

Der Fechtsportreferent:

Dr. Hoops

SS-Untersturmführer

Sr

Letter from Dr.Hoops to Herr Ehling sent on the day of Commemoration, the 9th November. Heydrich has asked Dr.Hoops to thank Ehling for agreeing to be a referee. He requests that Ehling meets in the guest room of the Hotel Rheinland, on the corner of Wilhelmstrasse, at 8.30pm on the 11th November so he can be issued with his referee's pass. Interestingly Dr.Hoops signs as the fencing sport consultant.

The 'Fördernde Mitglieder' monthly magazine for December 1936 proudly presented the success of th s first SS fencing championship. This magazine was available to supporting members of the SS that gave a monthly contribution. The costs involved for mounting such sporting events would be an excellent example of what the finances from the 'FM' (Supporting Members) organisation woulc be used for. Above, the impressive cover and below one of the inside pages relating to the article on the 1933 fencing championships.

Die erste SS-Fechtmeisterschaft

Der Kuppelsaal im Hause des Deutschen Sports während der Kämpfe

Die erste SS-Fechtmeisterschaft, die auf Befehl des Reichsführers SS durch die Sportgemeinschaft SS in Berlin vom 12. bis 14. November 1936 im Kuppelsaal des Hauses des Deutschen Sports zur Durchführung gelangte, sollte den Stand des Fechtens in der SS klar herausstellen, vor allem Auskunft geben über die Stärke unserer Besten und den Fortschritt unserer Anfänger.

Aus allen Teilen des Reiches hatten 180 SS-Männer in beiden Klassen (Meisterschaft Klasse A, Anfänger Klasse B) fast 300 Meldungen in den drei Waffen abgegeben.

Pünktlich zur festgesetzten Zeit begannen am 12. November morgens 9 Uhr die Kämpfe im Florett Klasse A. Durch die hohe Teilnehmerzahl waren hier nicht weniger als sieben Vorrunden nötig, zu denen noch fünf Vorrunden der Klasse B kamen. Über die Zwischen- und Vorendrunde gelangten in Klasse A acht Fechter in die Endrunde, in der SS-Oberscharführer Körner, SL-Hauptamt, der Beste war. In Klasse B setzte sich der Linkser SS-Bewerber Verlau, SS-Oberabschnitt Rhein, überlegen an die Spitze.

Das Degenfechten am zweiten Tage des Turniers hatte dadurch besondere Aufmerksamkeit, daß dieselbe Treffer-Anzeigevorrichtung in Tätigkeit trat, die zu den Olympischen Spielen benutzt wurde, und so konnte hier der Zuschauer jeden Treffer durch das Aufleuchten von Lampen genau verfolgen und sich über den Stand jedes Treffens zweier Gegner ein genaues Bild machen.

Die nicht so große Zahl der Degenfechter (rund 75) ermöglichte die Durchführung der Kämpfe ohne Vorendrunde, jedoch standen sich hier dafür in der Endrunde in beiden Klassen je 12 Fechter gegenüber. In Klasse A ging SS-Untersturmführer Kretschmann, Gestapo, als Sieger hervor. SS-Gruppenführer Heydrich, der seine Vor- und Zwischenrunde jedesmal als Sieger beendete, belegte den fünften Platz.

Siegerliste:

Florett Klasse A

1. Körner	O-Scharf.	SD-Hauptamt SS-Meister 1936
2. Lebacher	H-Scharf.	SS-OA Main
3. Roßner	U.-Scharf.	SD-Hauptamt
4. Baumann	Rottenführer	SD-OA-Ost
5. Kronenberg	St-Mann	SS-OA West
6. Timpe	St-Bew.	SS-OA Elbe
7. Plapp	O-Scharf.	SS-OA Südwest
8. Wendtland	Rottenführer	Sonder-Stuba. i. SS-Hauptamt

Degen Klasse A

1. Kretschmann	U-Stuf	SD-Hauptamt SS-Meister 1936
2. Plapp	O-Scharf.	SS-OA Südwest
3. Hildebrand	U-Stuf.	SD-Hauptamt
4. Schröder	O-Stuf.	SD-Hauptamt
5. Heydrich	Gruf.	SD-Hauptamt
6. Kroggel	U-Stuf.	SD-Hauptamt
7. Kronenberg	St-Mann	SS-OA West
8. Roßner	U-Scharf.	SD-Hauptamt

Säbel Klasse A

1. Hettmer	U-Scharf.	SS-OA Ost SS-Meister 1936
2. Körner	O-Scharf.	SD-Hauptamt
3. Heydrich	Gruf.	SD-Hauptamt
4. Liebscher	H-Scharf.	SS-OA Main
5. Roßner	St-Mann	SD-Hauptamt
6. Hainke	St-Mann	SD-Hauptamt
7. Timpe	St-Bew.	SS-OA Elbe
8. Raps	U-Scharf.	SS-OA Main

Florett Klasse B

1. Berlau	St-Bew.	SS-OA Rhein
2. Pause	St-Mann	SS-OA Elbe
3. Meyer-Mahndorf	H-Scharf.	SS-OA Nordwest
4. Schnabel	U-Scharf.	SS-OA Rhein
5. Haug	Anw.	SS-OA Südwest
6. Bruhns	U-Scharf.	SD-Hauptamt
7. Schlott	SS-Mann	SD-OA Süd
8. Jordan	U-Scharf.	SS-OA Main

Degen Klasse B

1. Haug	Anw.	SS-OA Südwest
2. Hettmer	U-Scharf.	SS-OA Ost
3. Simonsen	St-Mann	SS-OA West
4. Baumeler	Scharf.	SS-Germania
5. Oellig	SS-Mann	SS-OA West
6. Schenzler	Scharf.	SD-OA Südwest
7. Wätzig	O-Scharf.	SS-OA Süd
8. Rinow	SS-Mann	SD-Hauptamt

Säbel Klasse B

1. Schmitz	Rottenführer	SS-OA West
2. Meyer-Mahndorf	H-Scharf.	SS-OA Nordwest
3. Marquart	SS-Mann	SD-OA Süd
4. Zissow	SS-Mann	SD-OA Süd
5. Schnabel	U-Scharf.	SS-OA Rhein
6. Schlott	SS-Mann	SD-OA Süd
7. Legath	SS-Mann	SD-OA Süd
8. Domberg	St-Mann	SS-OA Südwest

The list of winners within their different classes from the 1936 SS fencing championships

Heydrich participated in two different classes both at class A (Master Class). With sword he came 5th over all and with sabre he came 3rd.

Der Reichsführer SS
Der Chef des Sicherheitshauptamtes

Berlin, den 7. Dezember 1936

An

Herrn E h l i n g.

Sehr geehrter Herr Ehling!

Für die der SS anlässlich ihrer diesjährigen Meisterschaft im Fechten erwiesene Unterstützung als Kampfrichter und Mitarbeiter spreche ich Ihnen meinen aufrichtigen Dank aus und überreiche Ihnen im Auftrage des Reichsführers SS eine Erinnerungsplakette.

H e i l H i t l e r !

Heydrich

SS - Gruppenführer.

Br

Letter from Heydrich to Herr Ehling sent on the 7th December. Heydrich thanks Ehling for acting as referee at the SS fencing championships and informs him that Reichsführer-SS Himmler has instructed Heydrich to tell Ehling that he will be presented with a special commemorative plaque.

emigrate to America. He also protected the Polish national team following the outbreak of hostilities.

After the German invasion of the Low Countries in May 1940, Paul Anspach, a Belgian, fell into the hands of the Gestapo who were investigating the murder of German deportees in Abbéville, Belgium. Anspach was cleared of any involvement in the crime, but not before it was noted that he was President of the International Fencing Federation (Fédération Internationale d'Escrime), based in Brussels. This information was immediately passed on to Heydrich in Berlin and he despatched SS-Untersturmführer Holzhauser to seize the archives of the FIE in Brussels.

Anspach was released, given a complete list of all the seized material and advised that everything had been sent to Berlin at the behest of SS-Gruppenführer Heydrich. Anspach appealed to the 'Reichssportführer' Reich Sports Leader) von Tschammer und Osten in an effort to regain the FIE property, Anspach was told that all the items would be returned as soon as possible and von Tschammer was ready to assist further if the archives were not back in Anspach's hands within the near future. Of course, nothing materialised, despite repeated requests. Both men had failed to understand Heydrich's true intentions; he had designs on the presidency of the FIE.

In December 1940, Heydrich was appointed to the highest German fencing office and was given responsibility for fencing in the Reich, under the National Socialist Reich Association for Physical Training, with effect from 1st January, 1941. No amount of complaining to the Reichssportführer by Anspach would tempt von Tschammer into upsetting the all powerful SS leadership.

Heydrich's new found situation in the world of fencing now placed him in a stronger position to address the erstwhile former prisoner of the Gestapo in Brussels, Paul Ansbach. On 5th February 1941, he summoned Anspach to the Prinz Albrecht Palace in Berlin. The Belgian vaguely remembered Heydrich from a brief meeting in 1935 when he was advised *"watch out, that man is dangerous, very dangerous"* [6]. These words must have been ringing in his ears when he was shown into an office in the imposing headquarters of the RSHA.

Seated behind a large desk was Reinhard Heydrich. On seeing Ansbach enter, Heydrich jumped up and cordially greeted him as one sportsman to another. After preliminary 'buttering up', Heydrich came to the point. He possessed all the documentation of the FIE and saw no reason why he should not immediately take over from Anspach as president; after all, his position had theoretically expired on 31st December and he was only still in office because the war had prevented a further election. Anspach was not impressed by this suggestion and rather bravely declined. Heydrich then proposed that the files remain in Berlin, offering Anspach full access at any time. Additionally, he suggested that two SS officers, Hoops and Talman, could act as liaison between Brussels and Berlin. The FIE President knew and respected both these men and nearly agreed to the terms, however after a twenty four hour delay, Anspach declined and surprisingly was allowed to return to his home unharmed [7].

Gone, but not forgotten, Anspach was soon to hear from Heydrich again. On 17th February, Talman delivered a letter which he requested Anspach to sign and return to Heydrich. The content was basically a request for Heydrich to temporarily take over the post of president until a final settlement could be reached at a later date.

Anspach reacted by sending a letter to Talman, (and forwarding a copy to the President of the International Olympic Committee) adamantly refusing any such hand over of his authority. However, Heydrich now played his trump card and formed an alliance with Dr. Basletta, a friend of Anspach and the Chairman of the Italian Fencing Association. In a letter dated 25th June, 1941, he stated:

"Dearest Mr. Anspach,
With regard to the management of the International Fencing Association, I have reached the following agreement with Dr. Basletta, the President of the Italian Fencing Association: for the duration of the war I shall carry on the direction of the affairs of the FIE in consultation with Dr. Basletta. The question of the ultimate direction of the FIE for the next period of office can only be settled after the end of the war. I have appointed SS-Hauptsturmführer Talman as my liaison officer with you" [8].

Another protest was sent to Heydrich by Anspach, but his declarations fell upon deaf ears. Heydrich had achieved his aim and did not even to reply to Anspach's letters. Possibly his attentions were now focused upon another battle further east; Operation Barbarossa, the invasion of the Soviet Union, had begun on 22nd June.

A lighthearted moment with Daluege. ...

....and a tense moment for the sportsman !

An excellent formal pose of Heydrich the fencer

‘ Heydrich with Allach fencer’
The famous painting by Vietze in 1941

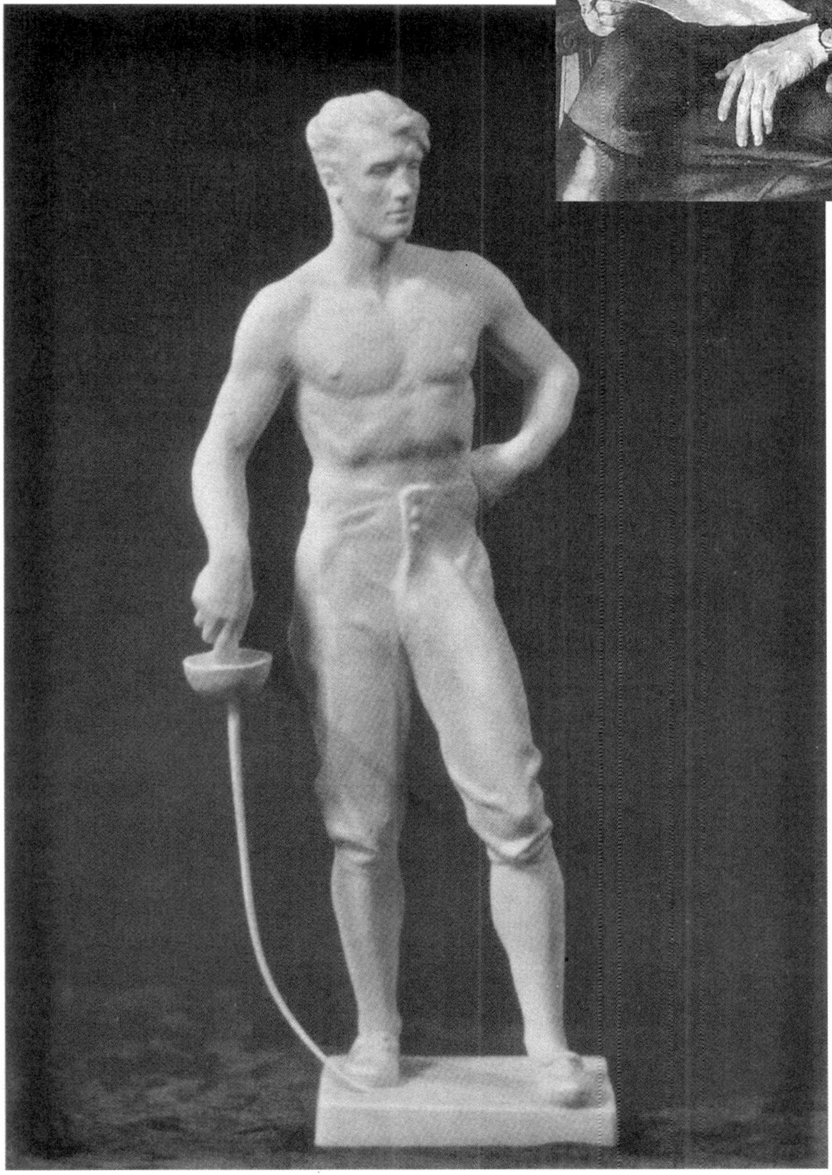

The fencer by Ottmar Obermeier, produced in white biscuit (unglazed) porcelain by the SS porcelain firm Allach-München GmbH. This beautifully sculptured figure must have pleased Heydrich.

CHAPTER 11
THE RSHA AND THE GERMAN POLICE SYSTEM

The International Criminal Police Organisation (Interpol) consisted of thirty-three countries, all co-operating in the fight against international crime. Heydrich, in his capacity as head of the German Criminal Police (Kripo), attended the Bucharest congress in March 1938. The seat of the organisation was in Vienna, where it was founded, however there was an attempt to transfer 'Interpol' to another country as a result of the German annexation of Austria, but this was defeated by the resistance of the German delegation. It was Heydrich's argument that the now deposed Austrian Secretary of State, Skubl, had been elected to the presidency for a term of five years and, as Austria was now a part of the German Reich, it should pass to Skubl's successor, SS-Brigadeführer Otto Steinhäusel, the Police President of Vienna. The opposition was soon defeated and Heydrich achieved his aim.

In June 1940, Steinhäusel died and Heydrich, (who's appetite for taking on new positions with the extra work they entailed seemed inexhaustable) immediately claimed the presidency for himself, eventually moving the seat of the organisation to Berlin-Wannsee. The 'Deutsche Allgemeine Zeitung' noted, *"The commission membership agreed that the successor had to originate from a state with the best organised police institutions. Without doubt this state is Germany. The request to take over the functions of the president of the commission was unanimous. The new president, SS-Gruppenführer Heydrich, has proven talent of organisation and energy for leadership of the German criminal police. He will show the international co-operation of criminal police offices which are now under his leadership, new ways of creating a powerful organisation to combat criminals and avoid crime"* [1]. Throughout the war, *Interpol* continued to operate successfully even though it's membership was slightly reduced by the withdrawal of Great Britain, France and some other smaller nations who had been 'annexed' by the Reich.

Arthur Nebe, Heydrich's subordinate and head of the 'Kripo', opened an Institute of Forensic Science in Berlin, which held related exhibitions. It attracted much interest from criminal police departments from around the world and many representatives visited the institute's buildings. Lina Heydrich states that her husband suspected a great number of these visitors were spies hoping to achieve an inside view of the Security Service. The exhibition included such things as tattoo designs of criminal fraternities, fingerprinting methods and the use of modern photography in assisting to detect and capture criminals. It was a great success and gained much praise from international police forces who drew on it's specialist knowledge.

There had always been an element of rivalry between the SD, which was a party organisation, and the Gestapo, a State organisation. In the 1935 restructuring of the SD, Heydrich failed to achieve suitable fields of activity which would differentiate between his two intelligence systems. Gestapo agents would often find themselves investigating the same areas as SD men. Consequently, in July 1937, Heydrich felt it necessary to specify their respective functions [2]. The SD was allotted science, Germanism and folk-lore, art, education, Party and State, constitution and administration, foreign countries, freemasonry and other miscellaneous societies. The Gestapo was given Marxism, treason and émigrés. The intention was clearly to avoid duplication. However, both remained responsible for Jews, churches, sects, other religious and ideological associations, pacifism, right-wing movements, other anti-State groups, economics and the press. Obviously, a certain amount of friction prevailed.

The young SD intellectuals were not content with what they saw as their fast diminishing role in the intelligence world since it appeared they were being relegated to the ideological spheres, (while the Gestapo reaped the benefits of handling the more tangible tasks). As a result, in an effort to promote it's position, the SD began to infiltrate the realm of the secret service, much to the annoyance of Canaris' Abwehr. On 21st December 1936, Canaris and Best signed an agreement, known as the 'Ten Commandments', which defined clearly the different roles of the Gestapo and the Abwehr [3]. The more the SD expanded into the field of secret intelligence, the more likely a showdown became likely.

The SD remained a collection bin for all the amateur spies of the type described in boys' comics. The embarrassing exploits of Heydrich's men during the Formis case only confirmed the inexperience of his department in the foreign intelligence network. Canaris believed the Tukhachevsky affair had been a double bluff by the Soviets and the gangster methods used by Heydrich's men could perhaps drag Germany into ruin. Canaris' biographer, Abshagen, contends that it was at this point when Canaris turned against both his former junior naval comrade, Heydrich and the Nazi regime [4]. After the Fritsch affair, Canaris was

Arthur Nebe, Heydrich's subordinate and head of the 'Kripo' (Criminal Police) opened an Institute of Forensic Sciences in Berlin. The institute created a lot of interest and attracted police departments from around the world. Many of their representatives visited the facility.

Representatives from the Spanish Police visit the Institute of Forensic Science. Reichsführer-SS Himmler and Heydrich attended this official visit. Here the Reichsführer shakes hands with Nebe at the entrance to the Institute in Berlin. Heydrich can be seen to the extreme right of the photograph.

Nebe and Heydrich explain the workings of the institute to the Spanish interpreter....

...and in turn, the interpreter outlines how the institute works.

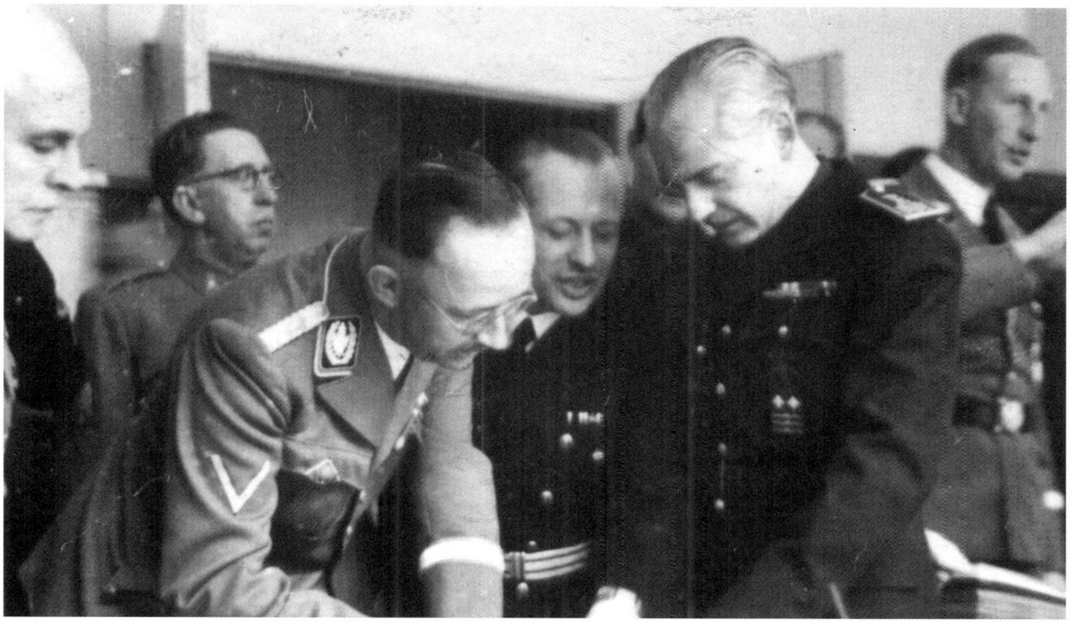

Following an initial outline, Reichsführer-SS Himmler discusses things in more detail, likewise Heydrich, seen here at the extreme right, also explains the nature of their work.

Later Heydrich describes the departmental structure to the Spanish guests. Nebe looks on.

The Reichsführer-SS Himmler addresses a conference on legal issues.

'The Legal Eagles'
Left to right: Daluege, Stuckart, Frank, Himmler, Heydrich, Best, Helldorf, unidentified.

among those calling for the downfall of Heydrich and Himmler. This did not, however, affect Canaris' personal view of Heydrich, Lina Heydrich mentioned post-war that the admiral mourned the death of his professional counterpart, stating, with tears in his eyes, that he had lost a good friend.

Following the order of Rudolf Hess on 9th June 1934, the SD had been the only permitted intelligence service of the NSDAP [5]. This was allowed on the grounds of the unwritten agreement that the SD would not interfere in Party matters, (it's brief was to detect enemies within the Party and not to snoop into Party affairs). Himmler had made a great effort to instruct his SD men not to participate in any discussions on internal matters and the reporting of such was strictly forbidden. However, there were two SD men whose ideas were rigorously opposed to this line.

Professor Reinhard Höhn was in charge of 'Zentralabteilung II 2' (Centre Unit II 2) in the 'SD Hauptamt' (SD Head Office) and his protégé, Otto Ohlendorf, was the director of his staff. It was their contention that researching the internal affairs of the NSDAP and reporting on the opinions and feelings of the populace was the fundamental reason for the establishment of the SD. In May 1936, at their first meeting, Höhn advised Ohlendorf that it was the task of the SD to inform the leading organisations of the Party and State about National Socialist developments and especially about wrong developments and tendencies [6]. Both men implicitly believed that they could influence the development of National Socialism. Höhn introduced a new concept of observation of 'spheres of life'. As Heinz Höhne explains, *"It was a sort of National Socialist version of the Gallup poll"* [7]. This was the birth of what became known as 'Meldungen aus dem Reich' (Reports from within the Reich). Ohlendorf remained responsible for these reports for years to come.

Ohlendorf's speciality was economics, but he soon expanded his area of reporting to include all aspects of the national life. Höhn was extremely pleased with the factual nature of his reports, but did not recognise the danger they posed as they became more and more critical, and began to awaken the wrath of some important Party members. In the summer of 1936, Höhn directed his criticism against a strong foe, Walther Frank, the National Socialist historian who had powerful friends. Julius Streicher, the Gauleiter in Franconia, rallied to his aid and produced some evidence of Höhn's hitherto unknown anti-National Socialist remarks. Höhn was dismissed and escaped to Sweden.

Ohlendorf then came under attack. Himmler began to distance himself from the young economist, describing him as 'Nazism's Knight of the Holy Grail'. Rudolf Brandt, Himmler's referent, describes Ohlendorf as *"not knowing how to cope with the Reichsführer. Really to get into contact with him he ought to bring him a rune stone from time to time and chat with him about his Germanic ideals. Instead of that, he's very cold and superior in his manner as he goes into some matter of which the Reichsführer has little knowledge"* [8]. Ohlendorf was reprimanded and told that his 'spheres of life' investigations were illegal. From then on he had to concentrate on economics. Ohlendorf asked to be relieved of his post, but Heydrich was in no mood to lose the intelligent young man from his staff.

The crisis caused by the Gestapo's mishandling of the Fritsch affair had placed Heydrich in a very vulnerable position and coupled with the loss of confidence in his SD, made Heydrich determined to restructure his organisations into one, well oiled machine; he formulated a plan for a Reich Security Service.

In the summer of 1938, Reichsführer-SS Himmler issued a decree aimed towards his great scheme, which was a fusion of the SS and police into a consolidated State Protection Corps. He proposed that members of the 'Ordnungspolizei' would join the SS and members of the 'Sicherheitspolizei' would join the Party organisation, the SD. Two years previously he had ordered that Commanders of the 'SD Oberabschnitte' would be nominated as Inspectors of the Sicherheitspolizei and SD. In 1937, he nominated Commanders of the 'SS Oberabschnitte' as Higher SS and Police Leaders in their respective military districts [9]. They would hold control of all police functions within their jurisdiction.

The SD was reliant on the Party for it's funding. Time and time again, the SD demanded more money from the Party's treasurer, Franz Xaver Schwarz, however even when tempted by increased promotion for himself within the SS, Schwarz was reluctant to release money. Hess' office frequently had to bail out the SD from it's financial embarrassment.

Heydrich commissioned Walter Schellenberg with the task of designing a new strategy for the security services under his command. Urgency became the name of the game as there were rumours that the SD was to be disbanded and as such Heydrich wished to remove the SD from the control of the Party, creating a new State organisation. Himmler realised that the loss of his intelligence service might promote the birth

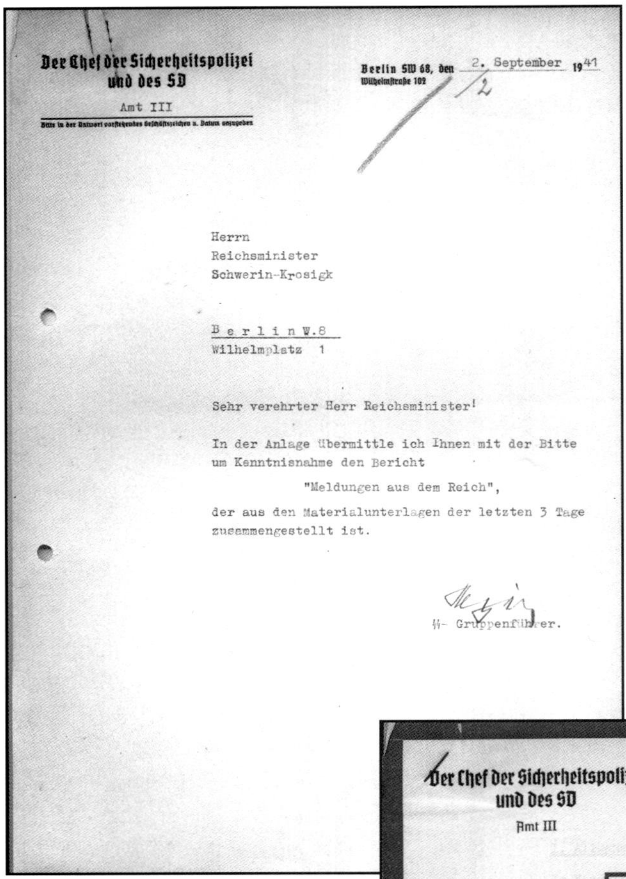

Der Chef der Sicherheitspolizei
und des SD

Amt III

Bitte in der Antwort vorstehendes Geschäftszeichen u. Datum anzugeben

Berlin SW 68, den 2. September 1941
Wilhelmstraße 102

Herrn
Reichsminister
Schwerin-Krosigk

B e r l i n W.8
Wilhelmplatz 1

Sehr verehrter Herr Reichsminister!

In der Anlage übermittle ich Ihnen mit der Bitte um Kenntnisnahme den Bericht

"Meldungen aus dem Reich",

der aus den Materialunterlagen der letzten 3 Tage zusammengestellt ist.

SS- Gruppenführer.

Der Chef der Sicherheitspolizei
und des SD

Amt III

Berlin SW 11, den 1. Sep. 1941
Prinz-Albrecht-Straße 8
für Rückfragen 120038/244

31

Geheim!

Persönlich - Sofort vorlegen!

Meldungen
aus dem Reich

Nr. 216

Vorliegender Bericht ist nur persönlich für den Adressaten bestimmt und enthält Nachrichtenmaterial, das der Aktualität wegen unüberprüft übersandt wird.

A surviving example of a 'Meldungen aus dem Reich' (Reports from within the Reich).
The information was gathered together by Otto Ohlendorf. Signed by Heydrich, this example was sent to Reichsminister Schwerin-Krosigk with a covering letter dated 2nd September 1941. This report was numbered '216'. The '31' typed near the top right was probably the report issue number.

PROMINENT MEMBERS OF THE NEW 'RSHA' (REICH SECURITY HEAD OFFICE)

A group of SD officers in conversation. Men such as these formed the nucleus of the new RSHA, under the command of early recruits from the SD. 2nd from right is Schellenberg, head of Foreign Intelligence and to his right stands Hermann Kluckhohn Heydrich's adjutant.

Bruno Streckenbach

Chief of Personnel

Heinrich Müller

Gestapo Chief

Otto Ohlendorf

The economics expert, and one of the most intelligent SD men. Ohlendorf was also the author of ‘Reports from the Reich’.

Dr.Rudolf Brandt

Himmler’s personal Assistant. He believed Ohlendorf did not understand Reichsführer-SS Himmler and as such the two men never got on well. Brandt described Ohlendorf as *“cold and superior in his manner”.*

of a rival from within the Party, with the consequent loss of the monopoly he treasured; with this in mind, he encouraged Heydrich's plans.

Heydrich envisaged combining the SD and 'Sicherheitspolizei' (Security Police), but the SD was to retain it's specialised character, and the SD staff would have improved pension rights. Schellenberg however was concerned that the new security service might be hampered by administrative lawyers. He believed that the new SD man must not be weighed down by laws of society or State and must also have complete freedom of movement. His views were strongly opposed by the old style lawyer, Werner Best. However Schellenberg had the support of his boss, Heydrich, and the two opposing camps prepared to do battle. In April 1939, Best published an article clearly attacking the Heydrich side [10], Heydrich was furious and ordered Schellenberg to reply. Best insisted that all men must be subject to the rules of state administration and the 'battle of words' continued to rage. Himmler's lack of confidence against the Party functionaries decided the outcome, (he was uncertain that the Party would accept a new super model of it's present SD) and the Schellenberg plan was dropped.

SS-Gruppenführer Heydrich

'Chef der Sicherheitspolizei und SD'
(Chief of the Security Police and Security Service)

Not to be defeated, Heydrich succeeded in creating a new 'Reichssicherheitshauptamt', or 'RSHA'. It's doors opening on 27th September 1939 [11]. but it was a diluted version of Heydrich's original dream. He remained it's head, but was not allowed to refer to it's existence officially outside the walls of the organisation. Heydrich was to be known as 'Chef der Sicherheitspolizei und SD' and this was also the heading used on all outside correspondence. Party and State refused to be mixed.

CHAPTER 12
ROAD TO WAR

"Eighty million people must obtain what is their right!" exclaimed Hitler at a military conference he held at the Obersalzberg on 22nd August 1939 [1]. Hitler was addressing his top admirals and generals in order to prepare them for the coming conflict which he declared was to commence on 'Y Day', Saturday 26th August, with the German invasion of Poland. With the knowledge that his bitterest enemy, the Soviet Union, would not move against him, he was prepared to risk war with the western powers of Europe in his first aggressive move eastwards, to establish his dream of 'living space' for the German people.

The origins of the Second World War can be traced to the terms imposed on Germany after her defeat in 1918. They have been examined in many authoritative works on the subject and therefore it is not necessary to go into them in great depth again for this particular study. Suffice to say, the National Socialist rise to power in the late twenties and early thirties would not have been so meteoric and may not have occurred at all, without the conditions imposed by the Allied powers at Versailles, which degraded the Germans, reducing them to nothing more than a second rate nation with no say in their future. Given the proud nature and strong belief in national honour of the German people, Versailles created a powder keg, waiting to explode and engulf the uneasy peace it had misguidedly built.

Adolf Hitler had made no secret of the fact that he wished to expand his national frontiers towards the vast open lands of the east. His objectives had been clearly explained in his monumental 'Mein Kampf', written while still a prisoner in Landsberg Prison, after his first unsuccessful attempt to gain power at the Munich Putsch of November 1923. An Austrian by birth, he always believed in the theory of the 'Greater Reich', a uniting together of all the German speaking people, regardless of nationality, under the umbrella of one united Germany. Hitler's own people, the Austrians would be the first to join the 'Greater Reich'.

In the summer of 1933, the Austrian Chancellor, Engelbert Dollfuss, banned the Austrian National Socialist Party, forcing many members to flee across the border into Bavaria. Many chose to join the SS in preference to the less disciplined SA. An Austrian Legion was formed under SS-Brigadeführer Alfred Rodenbucher. One such willing volunteer was an ex-sergeant major in the army, Fridolin Glass. He was the leader of a group of men who had been dismissed from the Austrian army, following the ban. Glass gained the confidence of SS-Gruppenführer Kurt Wittje, who supported the Austrian's idea of forming a new SS Standarte under his personal command. Himmler agreed, and Standarte 89, under the leadership of SS-Sturmbannführer Glass, was established in spring 1934.

The new leader of the Austrian SS-Standarte 89, Fridolin Glass decided that Dollfuss should be forced from office and conspired with others to bring about his downfall. On 25th July 1934, a group of Austrian SS men entered the Federal Chancellery and confronted Dollfuss. Not realising the precariousness of his situation, Dollfuss made an impatient gesture and was fatally shot by SS man Otto Planetta. Bleeding profusely and with only moments to live, the Chancellor began to discuss the situation with his captors. Even as he was dying, Dollfuss attempted to dissuade them from their course of action. Unsupported by the SA, the putschists soon failed in their attempt and were quickly arrested. Planetta and several others were executed, the remaining participants receiving long prison sentences [2].

There is little doubt that Hitler was aware of this coup, but maintained a safe distance to ensure he wouldn't be associated if the coup failed, however he was not prepared for the international backlash that ensued. Mussolini even mobilised troops near the Brenner Pass. A valuable lesson was learned, ensuring Hitler would never again allow such obvious moves against a foreign government, without some pretext for action beforehand.

The post-war author of a Heydrich biography, Calic positions Heydrich behind this coup. Indeed, Calic attempts to place all questionable manoeuvres by the Third Reich regime at the feet of the Security Chief, but in contrast to Calic's version of events, there is no direct evidence that Heydrich was involved.

There followed, in quick succession, a number of calculated and extremely dangerous moves by Hitler, in order to achieve his goal of bringing all German speaking people together within a new 'Reich' . In January 1935, Hitler regained the Saar by plebiscite. On 21st May, the same year, Hitler stated in a famous speech to the Reichstag, *"Germany needs peace and desires peace!..........Germany neither intends nor wishes to interfere in the internal affairs of Austria, to annex Austria, or to conclude an Anschluss"* [3]. France and

SS- Brigadeführer Alfred Rodenbucher

An Austrian Legion was formed under the command of Rodenbucher.

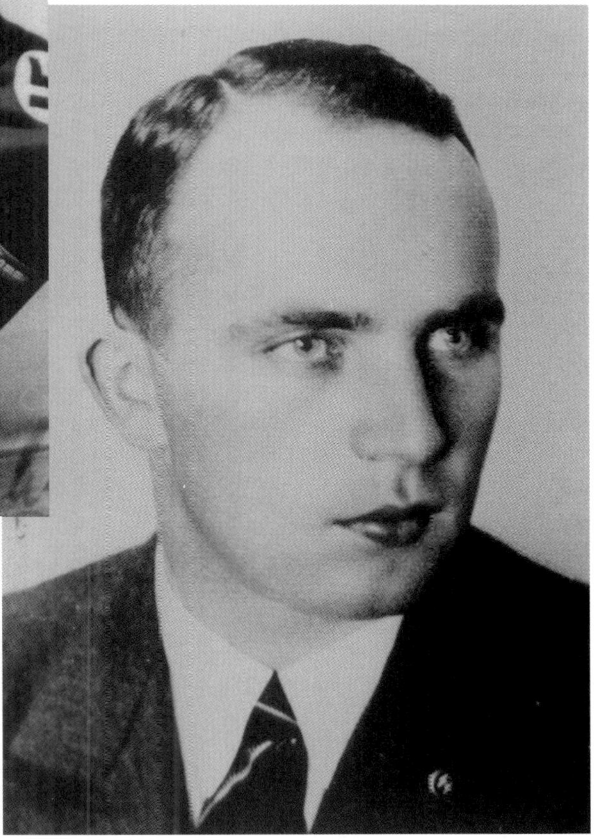

Fridolin Glass

Glass formed an SS Standarte in Spring 1934. It was members of Standarte 89 who confronted the Austrian Chancellor Dollfuss.

Above: Otto Planetta. He shot Chancellor Dollfuss

Right: The Austrian Chancellor Engelbert Dollfuss. Dollfuss was shot by Planetta on the 25th July 1934,Planetta was subsequently executed. Schuschnigg took over as Chancellor.

Great Britain sat back and watched events. Mussolini now decided to exercise his expansion muscles and attacked Abyssinia on 3rd October 1935. The German re-occupation of the Rhineland followed in March 1936, a direct act in breach of the Versailles Treaty. Still nobody acted.

The Austrian Chancellor, Kurt von Schuschnigg, taking Hitler at his word following the Reichstag speech, concluded an agreement with the German Government on 11th July 1936. The Austrians made several concessions and Schuschnigg felt relaxed with his new false security. Five days later, an episode began that would provide both Hitler and Mussolini with the chance to try their armed forces in battle, the Spanish civil war burst onto the world stage. 1937 proved to be a quiet twelve months, but the 1938 New Year celebrations were still fresh in people's minds when Hitler once again provided the international headlines.

Following the assassination of Dollfuss, the Austrian National Socialists were targeted by the police. Hitler was not pleased to hear of the continual police pressure being placed on his supporters, many of which, had been so persecuted that they were living in hiding. Some spent months living in caves to avoid detection, those caught found themselves in 'concentration camp' style prisons such as the one at Wöllersdorf. Bombings and general unrest began to occur in the Austrian capital at an alarming rate. The situation deteriorated to such an extent that the German ambassador in Vienna, von Papen, managed to arrange a personal interview for Schuschnigg with Hitler.

Dr.Arthur Seyss-Inquart

Seyss-Inquart talking with Hitler whilst Himmler and Heydrich look on.
Seyss-Inquart was nominated as Hitler's representative.

On the 12th February 1938, Hitler and Schuschnigg met at the Obersalzberg. Hitler immediately gave his ultimatum. The ban on the National Socialists was to be lifted, Dr. Seyss-Inquart and Glaise-Horstenau, both ardent National Socialists, were to be appointed to the government and all jailed supporters were to be released under an amnesty. Failure to comply would result in an immediate invasion. Schuschnigg, realising that he would be handing over Austria's independence to Hitler, hesitated. Finally, after several calculated threats, he signed and returned across the border, a broken man.

Chancellor Kurt von Schuschnigg

Chancellor of Austria after Dollfuss was shot in 1934, Schuschnigg tried to gain support around Europe without success. He finally resigned in 1938.

Dr. Seyss-Inquart (centre) and Glaise-Horstenau (below) were both ardent National Socialists and respected by Hitler. With the worsening political situation in Austria, Chancellor Schuschnigg met with Hitler and was told that Seyss-Inquart and Glaise-Horstenau were to be appointed to the government. Schuschnigg agreed and then renaged on the agreement, subsequently he resigned from office, paving the way for the National Socialists.

The Austrian National Socialists were forced underground after the death of Dollfuss. Many spent periods in caves to prevent capture by the Police, others escaped to Germany. Politics continued and the printing of the Austrian National Socialist newspaper or any other activity from a National Socialist viewpoint had to be continued in secret.

For those National Socialists caught actively engaging in politics,there was always Wöllersdorf Prison, where many were detained.

Once back on his own territory, Schuschnigg had time to reflect on his decision and decided to hold a plebiscite of his people. Surely, this would convince the international community that the Austrians did not wish German domination? Hitler was furious. Göring demanded Schuschnigg's resignation and his replacement by Seyss-Inquart. Meanwhile, Hitler obtained assurances from the Duce that he would not interfere. Schuschnigg searched Europe for support, without success and was eventually forced to resign. After some resistance from the Austrian President Wilhelm Miklas, Hitler at last achieved his dream of unification. On 12th March 1938, he crossed the border at Braunau and Austria ceased to exist.

Meanwhile the Himmler-Heydrich machine was preparing for the occupation of Austria. Heydrich had long since drawn up a list of opponents, appointing his SD officials to posts in the forthcoming security departments throughout Austria in readiness. He accompanied Himmler to Vienna at once to oversee the measures required to ensure a peaceful transition of government. Gestapo Chief Müller and Dr. Stahlecker both took up office in the Austrian capital. 'Protective custody arrest' was a phrase with which some Austrians became all too familiar. Schuschnigg was no exception. He again crossed what had been the old Austro-German frontier and which now no longer existed, but this time Schuschnigg was escorted by the Gestapo; his destination was Dachau.

Among Himmler's reception committee at Aspern, the Vienna airport, at three in the morning of 12th March, were Ernst Kaltenbrunner, Odilo Globocnik and Michael Skubl, the Austrian Chief of Police. Kaltenbrunner, was later to replace the subject of this work as head of the RSHA, Globocnik was later to direct 'Aktion Reinhard' in Poland and Skubl, the President of 'Interpol', was, within a few days, under arrest. By the end of the year, the need to send Austrian political prisoners across the non-existent border to Germany had disappeared. Himmler had quickly selected a site for a new concentration camp in the neighbourhood of the Wienergraben, a massive quarry near the picturesque village of Mauthausen. Franz Ziereis was appointed as commandant and both Himmler and Heydrich now had the first opportunity to exercise their powers in a foreign land.

Next, on Hitler's agenda, was Czechoslovakia. Following the capitulation in 1918, a new Republic of Czechoslovakia had been born from the ruins of the Habsburg Empire, under the presidency of Tomáš Masaryk, one of it's founders. Masaryk had been assisted by the talented son of a peasant, Eduard Beneš, who had succeeded Masaryk in 1935, to become the country's second President. The multi-national fabric of the new Czechoslovakian state created problems from it's inception. One million Hungarians, half a million Ruthenians and three and a quarter million Sudeten Germans all looked to their 'mother' countries and desired greater autonomy. Aside from these minorities, the Slovaks also longed for enhanced liberty.

The Sudeten crisis of summer 1938, was largely engineered by Hitler as an alternative to obvious aggression against Czechslovakia. "Case Green", the invasion of Czechoslovakia, had been formulated in 1937 by Werner von Blomberg, however as events transpired, it was not to be used. The German Foreign Minister, SS- Gruppenführer Joachim von Ribbentrop, was left in the cold. Under Hitler's orders, SS-Obergruppenführer Werner Lorenz, the head of 'VOMI' (the department for racial Germans abroad), opened negotiations with Konrad Henlein, the leader of the Sudeten Germans [4].

Henlein, a gymnasium teacher, headed the Sudeten Party and had the backing of the 'Kameradschaftbund', a secret society which followed the doctrine of the Austrian Catholic philosopher, Othmar Spann. The Spann circle came under the watchful eye of the SD [5] and had joined the ranks of those organisations which were viewed by Heydrich as 'not operating within the interests of the German Reich'. Catholic extremists and Freemasons were high on Heydrich's list. Following the Anschluss, Spann had been arrested and was detained in a concentration camp. Henlein was personally distrusted by Heydrich, being suspected of weak German nationalist beliefs, certain other leading members of his Sudeten Party were also suspected of favouring a course which did not include becoming part of the 'Greater Reich'.

Heydrich resolved to bring down Henlein and therefore allied himself with Henlein's main political adversary within the Sudeten German Party, Karl Hermann Frank (Frank had been the leader of the Sudeten National Socialist Party which had been dissolved and absorbed into the Sudeten Nationalist Movement under Henlein). This was an alliance which would last, and resulted in Frank playing a leading role in Bohemia-Moravia under Heydrich, meanwhile Heydrich ordered Henlein to be watched constantly and the SD office in Dresden was to co-ordinate the operation.

Henlein had established contacts with the British Foreign Office and was twice invited to visit London. He also kept his options with the Czech Government open, Heydrich feared that he would sell out to the

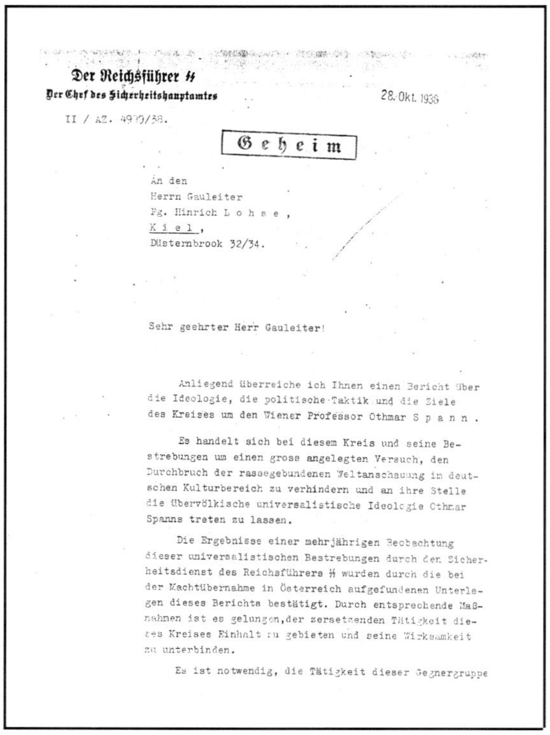

Der Reichsführer SS
Der Chef des Sicherheitshauptamtes

28. Okt. 1938

II / AZ. 49[illegible]/38.

G e h e i m

An den
Herrn Gauleiter
Pg. Hinrich L o h s e ,
K i e l ,
Düsternbrook 32/34.

Sehr geehrter Herr Gauleiter!

Anliegend überreiche ich Ihnen einen Bericht über die Ideologie, die politische Taktik und die Ziele des Kreises um den Wiener Professor Othmar S p a n n .

Es handelt sich bei diesem Kreis und seine Bestrebungen um einen gross angelegten Versuch, den Durchbruch der rassegebundenen Weltanschauung im deutschen Kulturbereich zu verhindern und an ihre Stelle die übervölkische universalistische Ideologie Othmar Spanns treten zu lassen.

Die Ergebnisse einer mehrjährigen Beobachtung dieser universalistischen Bestrebungen durch den Sicherheitsdienst des Reichsführers SS wurden durch die bei der Machtübernahme in Österreich aufgefundenen Unterlagen dieses Berichts bestätigt. Durch entsprechende Maßnahmen ist es gelungen, der zersetzenden Tätigkeit dieses Kreises Einhalt zu gebieten und seine Wirksamkeit zu unterbinden.

Es ist notwendig, die Tätigkeit dieser Gegnergruppe

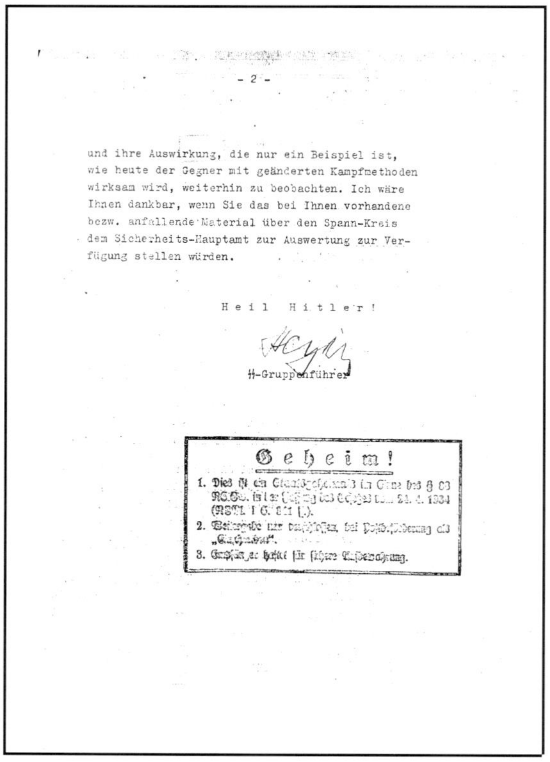

\- 2 -

und ihre Auswirkung, die nur ein Beispiel ist, wie heute der Gegner mit geänderten Kampfmethoden wirksam wird, weiterhin zu beobachten. Ich wäre Ihnen dankbar, wenn Sie das bei Ihnen vorhandene bzw. anfallende Material über den Spann-Kreis dem Sicherheits-Hauptamt zur Auswertung zur Verfügung stellen würden.

H e i l H i t l e r !

SS-Gruppenführer

G e h e i m !

1. Dies ist ein [illegible] ... 24. 4. 1934 [illegible]
2. [illegible]
3. [illegible]

Important secret document from Heydrich to Gauleiter Lohse dated 28th October 1938. The document discusses the political tactics and goals of Professor Othmar Spann. Spann and his followers believed in a 'super-national' view of politics not 'hindered' by the constraints of nationalism or nationalities. Heydrich found evidence of the circle's subversive activities and managed to stop them. Worries about any continued activities from them meant that Heydrich needed to keep them under observation. In this document, Heydrich asks Lohse to supply any information about the Spann circle for analysis by the 'Sicherheits-Hauptamt' (Security Service Head Office).

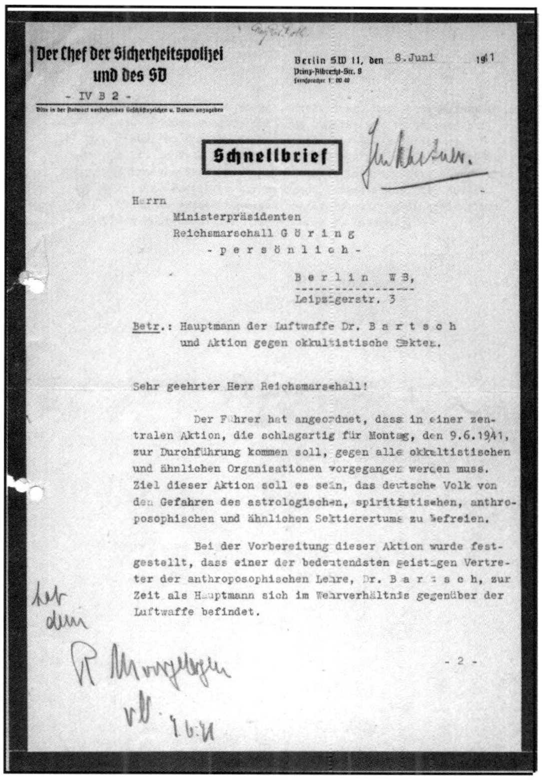

Der Chef der Sicherheitspolizei
und des SD
- IV B 2 -
Bitte in der Antwort vorstehendes Geschäftszeichen u. Datum anzugeben

Berlin SW 11, den 8. Juni 1941
Prinz-Albrecht-Str. 8
Fernsprecher 1 00 40

Schnellbrief

Herrn
Ministerpräsidenten
Reichsmarschall G ö r i n g
- p e r s ö n l i c h -

B e r l i n W 8,
Leipzigerstr. 3

Betr.: Hauptmann der Luftwaffe Dr. B a r t s c h
und Aktion gegen okkultistische Sekten.

Sehr geehrter Herr Reichsmarschall!

Der Führer hat angeordnet, dass in einer zentralen Aktion, die schlagartig für Montag, den 9.6.1941, zur Durchführung kommen soll, gegen alle okkultistischen und ähnlichen Organisationen vorgegangen werden muss. Ziel dieser Aktion soll es sein, das deutsche Volk von den Gefahren des astrologischen, spiritistischen, anthroposophischen und ähnlichen Sektierertums zu befreien.

Bei der Vorbereitung dieser Aktion wurde festgestellt, dass einer der bedeutendsten geistigen Vertreter der anthroposophischen Lehre, Dr. B a r t s c h, zur Zeit als Hauptmann sich im Wehrverhältnis gegenüber der Luftwaffe befindet.

- 2 -

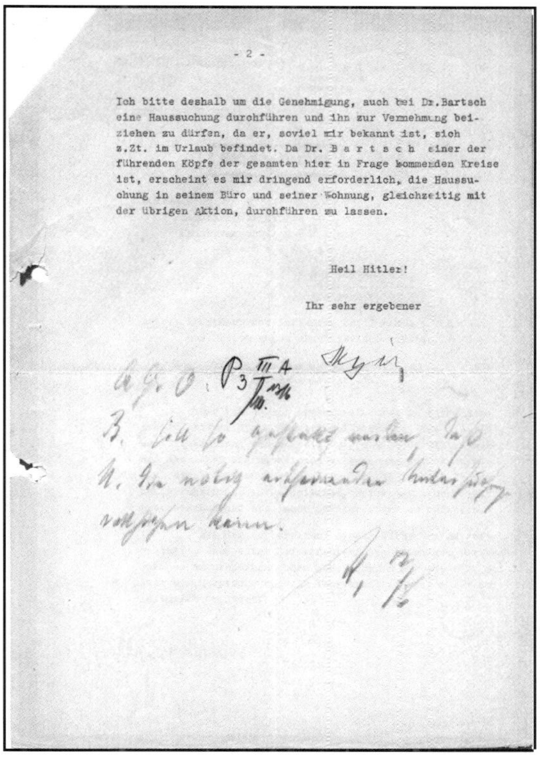

- 2 -

Ich bitte deshalb um die Genehmigung, auch bei Dr. Bartsch eine Haussuchung durchführen und ihn zur Vernehmung beiziehen zu dürfen, da er, soviel mir bekannt ist, sich z.Zt. im Urlaub befindet. Da Dr. B a r t s c h einer der führenden Köpfe der gesamten hier in Frage kommenden Kreise ist, erscheint es mir dringend erforderlich, die Haussuchung in seinem Büro und seiner Wohnung, gleichzeitig mit der übrigen Aktion, durchführen zu lassen.

Heil Hitler!

Ihr sehr ergebener

Heydrich kept a watchful eye on all secret organisations, for example, the Catholic Spann circle (which backed Henlein), Freemasonry and even obsure groups such as occultists. In this document sent to Göring by Heydrich on the 8th June 1941, Heydrich asks for permission to search the house of Luftwaffe Hauptmann Dr.Bartsch. He was known to Heydrich as a leading member within spiritualist circles. Interestingly Hitler ordered this 'clamp down' on occultists,astrologers, spiritualists, etc. deeming them a dangerous influence on the German people.

Hitler the new leader of a combined Austro-German Greater Reich is driven through Salzburg, just after unification on the 12th March 1938

Reichsführer-SS Himmler and Heydrich in Vienna just after the unification of Austria and Germany on the 12th March 1938.

Eduard Beneš

President of Czechoslovia from 1935. He resigned on the 5th October 1938, Dr.Emil Hacha took his place.

Werner Lorenz

Head of 'VOMI', the department for racial Germans abroad.

Konrad Henlein

Leader of the Sudeten German Party. Heydrich did not trust Henlein and allied himself with Karl Hermann Frank.

Karl Hermann Frank

Frank was trusted by Heydrich in preference to Henlein. The two remained friendly even after Heydrich was appointed Acting-Reichsprotektor of Bohemia-Moravia by Hitler, a position that Frank expected for himself.

Prague administration. Beneš was, however, uncompromising and refused to concede an inch of autonomy. The pressure on Henlein increased and conceiving a possible defeat at the hands of the Heydrich-Frank coalition, Henlein pre-empted his foes by collaborating with the one person who could save his position, Hitler. The SD was instructed not to pursue any further action against Henlein.

Hitler's position, now reinforced by the backing of the main party in the Sudetenland, was such that he could move against the Prague Government. First, however, in early May 1938, Hitler paid a visit on his ally, Mussolini, in Rome. Accompanying Hitler within his vast retinue of generals, Party functionaries and diplomats, were the now seemingly inseparable pair, Himmler and Heydrich. Hitler's Axis partner was apparently appraised of his intentions towards Czechoslovakia. On his return to Berlin, Hitler increased the political pressure on Beneš, speaking out in defence of the German minority, who were said to be constantly the victims of unfair treatment. Rumours of an imminent German invasion against Czechoslovakia abounded. Much to Hitler's surprise, the Czech Government ordered a partial mobilisation on 20th May 1938 [6]. Both Great Britain and France made half-hearted references to their obligations to Prague, supported by the Soviet Union. Hitler hesitated. In time, he regained his impetus and viewed this new situation as a minor setback. However, 'Case Green', the invasion of Czechoslovakia, was to go ahead on the revised date of 1st October 1938 and plans were set in motion.

Intent upon increasing the tension, Hitler proceeded to hold manoeuvres near the Czech border in June 1938. He encouraged Henlein to place the Czechs in a confrontational situation and fed the greed of their neighbours, Poland and Hungary. Meanwhile, France and Great Britain pressed for Beneš to make concessions. On 7th September, the London Times proposed ceding the Sudetenland to the Reich. In his speech to round off the 'Reichsparteitage' (Reich Party Days held at Nuremberg) on 12th September, Hitler made clear his intentions: *".....The Germans of Czechoslovakia are neither defenceless or deserted. Let this be noted"* [7]. These words resulted in riots in the Sudetenland, causing the deaths of three hundred people. Preparations for war were under way.

Once again, Hitler was taken by surprise. The British Prime Minister, Neville Chamberlain, dispatched a message to Berchtesgaden on the night of the thirteenth, proposing that he would be willing to travel to any place in order to meet Hitler and discuss the situation. Hitler reluctantly agreed, but insisted that the Prime Minister should fly to Berchtesgaden for the conference. Chamberlain arrived at the 'Berghof' on the afternoon of 15th September 1938.

Hitler quickly came to the point, demanding the annexation of the Sudeten territories, there was no compromise and unless his demands were met, the alternative would be war. The entire matter would be left with Chamberlain and his cabinet to decide, Hitler added that Great Britain should recognise the right of the Sudeten minority to self-determination and reminded Chamberlain that this was a principal created by the Versailles Treaty in 1919. Chamberlain agreed to return to Great Britain in order to discuss the matter with the Cabinet. In reply, Hitler promised to postpone any immediate military action.

There followed many exchanges of diplomatic notes between the governments of France, Great Britain and Czechoslovakia. Ambassadors and embassy staff worked overtime in the three capitals. The result was that the two western powers were not prepared to go to war to support the eastern European democracy. Russia was ready to fight, but only on condition that France would also. Beneš had little option, but to acquiesce to the wishes of his so called allies.

Chamberlain returned to Germany on 22nd September 1938, meeting Hitler at the Hotel Dreesen in Bad Godesberg. He gave his host the startling news that Great Britain, France and even Czechoslovakia agreed to the cession of the Sudetenland. Chamberlain also proposed the existing treaties between France, the Soviet Union and Czechoslovakia be dissolved in favour of an international guarantee. Hitler, not expecting a complete folding of all resistance to his plans, had to quickly re-think his strategy. After an embarrassing pause, he stated that recent events had altered the stakes, he would not be willing to agree to Chamberlain's proposals as they stood at present. Now he required not just the Sudetenland but Czechoslovakia in its entirety. The Prime Minister obtained a memorandum on Hitler's demands and left for home, just as news reached them that the Czechs had mobilised their army.

War seemed inevitable. The British Cabinet rejected Hitler's proposals, as did the Prague Government with a new found air of bravado. London, Paris and Prague prepared for war. On 26th September, Hitler, having again found his proposals unacceptable to the now intransigent western governments, became enraged. He shouted furiously at Sir Horace Wilson, Chamberlain's confidential adviser, *"There's no point in going on with negotiations. The Germans are being treated like niggers; nobody dares to treat even Turkey this way! On 1st October I'll have Czechoslovakia where I want her"* [8]. He then set a deadline for the acceptance of all his terms: 2pm on 28th September 1938.

After calming down, Hitler agreed to a crisis conference in Munich between Great Britain, Germany, France and the eleventh hour mediator, Italy. No mention was made of representation by Czechoslovakia.

At 12.30pm on 29th September, Hitler greeted the heads of government in the 'Führerbau', at the Königsplatz, Munich. Earlier that day, he had travelled to Kufstein to meet Mussolini. The Italian dictator was handed a copy of Hitler's proposals and asked to present them as his own. The 'Duce' was only too willing to agree, realising that if war began, he was honour bound to support his Axis partner. The final upshot of this affair was that Czechoslovakia was abandoned to the Germans. Hitler achieved his objective and the world breathed a sigh of relief. The 'Munich Agreement', as it became known, although dated 29th September 1938, was duly signed in the small hours of the morning of the 30th [9].

The British head of government called on Hitler in his private apartment at Prinzregentenplatz later on the 30th and asked him to countersign a 'gentlemen's agreement' confirming both governments desire never to go to war with one another again. On his return to England Chamberlain held this piece of paper aloft at Heston Airport, declaring "peace in our time" [10], it was ironic that a year later Britain would declare war on Germany.

On the 3rd October 1938, Hitler crossed the border into the Sudetenland in the footsteps of his troops. Heydrich was again able to set up SD and Gestapo units in the newly acquired territory. Captured documents, produced post-war at Nuremberg by the Russians, proved that these units had originally been intended, under the terms of 'Case Green', to act as 'Einsatzgruppen' (Special Action groups), but took on a more placid role, owing to the peaceful nature of the 'invasion'.

President Beneš resigned on 5th October 1938 and flew into exile, being provisionally substituted by General Sirovy. Who in turn, was replaced by the ageing Dr. Emil Hácha, the Chief Justice of the Supreme Court. Hácha was sixty-six years old, well intentioned, but rather weak, he ascended to the Presidency of what was left of Czecho-Slovakia (now officially spelt with a hyphen) on the 30th November 1938,

Within days of his occupation of the Sudetenland, Hitler was planning to take over the remnants of Czecho-Slovakia. He planned to re-occupy the Memel region, lost to Lithuania at Versailles, and also to occupy Danzig, a thorn in the German side since the aforementioned treaty had cut the old Reich in two with the 'Polish Corridor'. Encouraging the Slovak nationalists to press for independence, he hoped to break up what remained of Masaryk's dream.

By 13th March 1939, bowing to pressure from both within and outside his borders, Hácha visited Hitler in the new Reich Chancellery in Berlin. He placed his country in the hands of the Führer, but requested that she be granted the right to her own national existence, Hitler replied that his troops would enter the Czech homeland within four hours. Hácha was astonished that Hitler had given him such short notice and could not see how armed Czech resistance could be forestalled in that limited time. He was allowed to telephone Prague, but to the shock of those gathered around him, he suffered a suspected heart attack. Panicking that the world would suspect murder, Doctor Morell was hastily summoned and was surprisingly able to revive the President. Consequently the authorities in Prague were ordered not to provide any resistance to the invader, and a little before 4am on 14th March 1939, Czecho-Slovakia also ceased to exist.

At 9am the same morning, German troops entered Prague followed soon after by Hitler. He was presented to German students in the company of Himmler, Heydrich and Wolff. Such a strong SS presence was a prelude to the capital later becoming an SS dominated city. Below the Führer Standard, at a window of the Hradcany Castle, Hitler looked out at the cheering Sudetens. This was the first time German troops had occupied an area that did not boast a German majority.

By the time the French and British governments handed notes of protest to the German Foreign Ministry via their respective embassies in Berlin, Hitler had created the Protectorate of Bohemia-Moravia and sent troops to assist in the defence of the 'independent' Slovakia. For the position of Reichsprotektor, Hitler appointed the former Minister for Foreign Affairs, Baron Constantin von Neurath. Meanwhile Heydrich installed his men in the Bohemian capital, Dr. Walter Stahlecker having been commissioned with the task of Chief of Security Police for the Protectorate.

Chamberlain is greeted at Munich Airport on the 29th September 1938 by Ritter von Epp, von Ribbentrop and von Eberstein.

Chamberlain is given a warm welcome with formal 'pomp and ceremony' ronicallyfor what was a 'crisis meeting'

Left to right: Wagner, von Epp, Daluege, von Ribbentrop, Heydrich, Chamberlain and Fiehler

On the 29th Seprember 1938 under the watchful gaze of Bismark, the negotiators discuss the future of Czechoslovakia within the'Führerbau', Munich. Left, Hitler next to (back to camera) Mussolini. Left of the fireplaceChamberlain confers with Horace Wilson. Right (facing camera) von Ribbentrop and von Weizsäcker.

Chamberlain signs the' Munich Agreement' officially on the 29th september 1938, but actually in the small hours of the next morning, assisted by Julius Schaub.

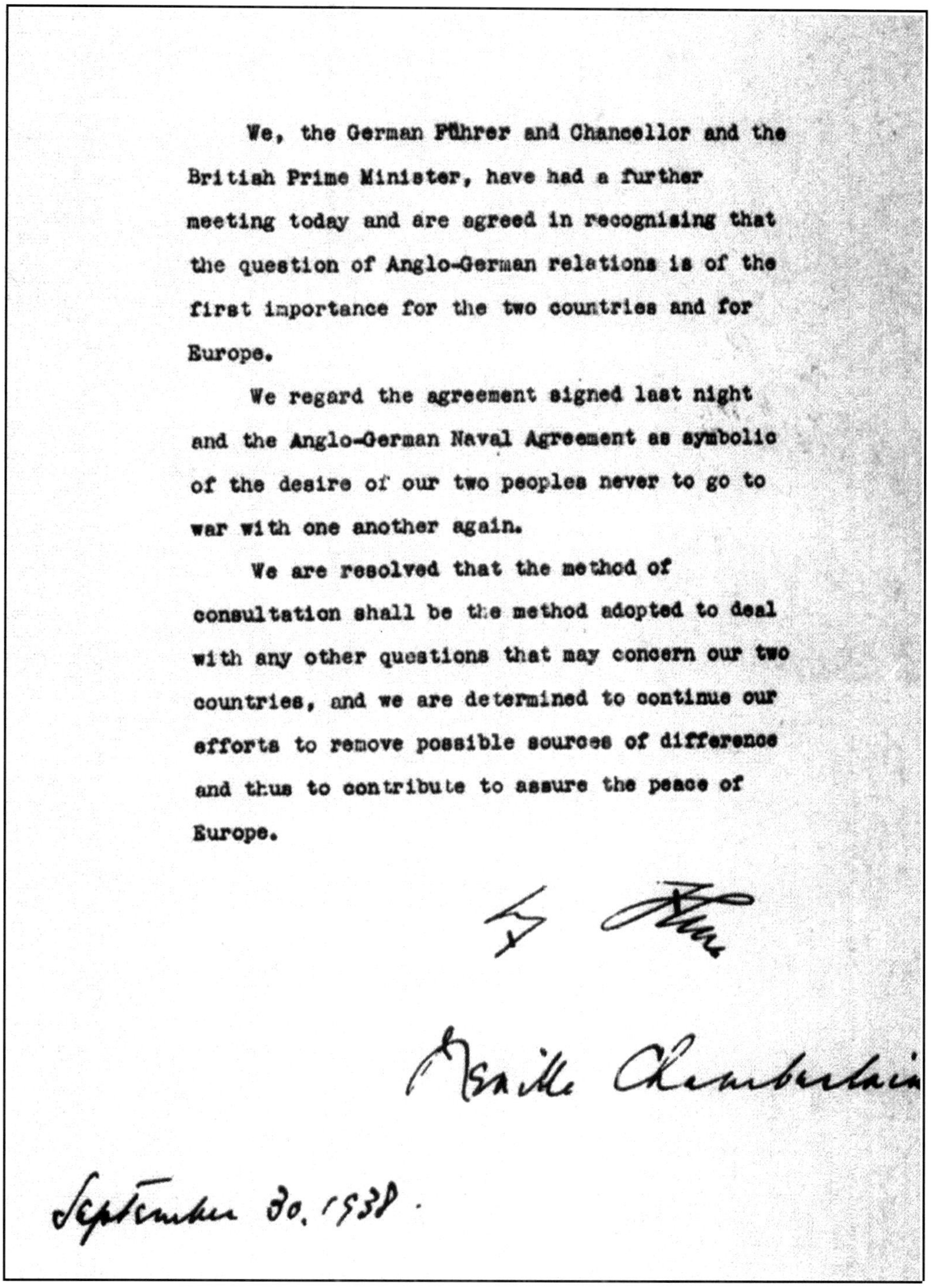

We, the German Führer and Chancellor and the British Prime Minister, have had a further meeting today and are agreed in recognising that the question of Anglo-German relations is of the first importance for the two countries and for Europe.

We regard the agreement signed last night and the Anglo-German Naval Agreement as symbolic of the desire of our two peoples never to go to war with one another again.

We are resolved that the method of consultation shall be the method adopted to deal with any other questions that may concern our two countries, and we are determined to continue our efforts to remove possible sources of difference and thus to contribute to assure the peace of Europe.

Neville Chamberlain

September 30. 1938.

The 'Gentlemen's agreement' signed by both Hitler and Chamberlain, that stated their governments desire never to go to war with each other again. This was the agreement that Chamberlain historically waved at Heston Airport on his return to England. Ironically the British government declared war on Germany the following year. A surprised Hitler had to cancel the 1939 yearly National Rally held at Nuremberg The 'Reichsparteitage' or National Party Rally was destined to be held that same month.

Dr.Emil Hacha

A supreme court judge, who took on the unenviable position of President of the Czech-Republic.

Hitler waits to sign the proclamation declaring the new Reichprotectorate of Bohemia Moravia in March 1939. Left to right: Bormann, Hitler, Frick, Lammers andStuckart.

Chamberlain arrives back in England

The famous wave of the "gentlemen's agreement" paper at Heston Airport by Chamberlain. The document had been signed by Hitler and Chamberlain on the 30th September 1938

Above: From a window of the Hradschin in Prague, the Führer, Adolf Hitler looks out at the applauding crowds

Right: Sudeten Germans crowd the Hradschin for a glimpse of their 'Führer', March 1939

Adolf Hitler meets Sudeten German Students in the courtyard of the Hradschin in March 1939 shortly after German troops had entered Prague, Reichsführer-SS Himmler, Heydrich and Wolff can be seen directly behind him.

The German Foreign Minister, von Ribbentrop

von Ribbentrop informed his Polish counterpart, Beck, that Germany demanded the return of Danzig to the German State.

Baron Constantin von Neurath

Hitler appointed von Neurath as Reichsprotector for Bohemia-Moravia.

Der Reichsführer SS
Der Chef des Sicherheitshauptamtes
I 12

Archiv 55 253/37 Hun/Elb.

Berlin, 20. Januar 1939

An
Reichsführer SS

Berlin SW 11
Prinz-Albrecht-Str.8.

Betr.: D a v i d , Herbert, Dr., Rechtsanwalt,
wohnh.: bisher in Leitmeritz, dzt. in Reichenberg.

Vorg.: Dort. Schrb. Tgb.-Nr. A/6/92/38 u. A/19/177/38 - vom 3.11.1938,
hies. Schrb. Archiv 55 253/37 vom 19.11. und 2o.12 1938.

Dr. Herbert D a v i d ist alter Nationalsozialist. Bei allen innervölkischen Auseinandersetzungen des Sudetendeutschtums hat er weltanschaulich stets eine saubere Linie gewahrt.

D. ist jetzt Reichstagsabgeordneter und bekleidet im Stabe des Gauleiters und Reichskommissars Konrad Henlein eine führende Stellung.

Als Freimaurer ist D. hier nicht erfaßt.

Persönlicher Stab RF SS | Anlagen
Eingang: 25. Jan. 19
Tgb.Nr.: A 6/92/38.
an: RF

F. K. 8. 38. 100000.

Document dated 20th January 1939 to Reichsführer-SS Himmler from Heydrich on the 'Chef des Sicherheitshauptamtes' letter heading. The document details that Dr.Herbert David from the Sudetenland is an old National-Socialist and with respect to all internal Sudetenland matters has always maintained an ideologically clean stance. Heydrich confirms that David is a leading member of Gauleiter Henlein's staff, and has no evidence indicating of David being a Freemason. This document shows clearly the importance such issues were to both Heydrich and Himmler, even during the crucial months of 1939.

On 23rd March 1939, Hitler annexed the Baltic area of Memel, reversing yet another 'crime' of the Versailles Treaty. However, Hitler had already decided on a much bigger prize, the German city of Danzig, on the Baltic coast, which had been declared a Free State under the protection of the League of Nations. To provide Poland with access to the sea, a wide strip of territory was cut through the German heartland and handed to the Poles in 1919, it became known as the 'Polish Corridor' and was probably the one act that outraged the German people more than the other terms forced upon them by the Treaty.

Von Ribbentrop informed the Polish Foreign Minister, Beck, that Germany demanded the return of Danzig to it's rightful position within the German State and suggested that the corridor be crossed by a highway and railroad, under German control. Not surprisingly, the Poles rejected Hitler's plans. Warsaw was not prepared to be as easily manipulated as Vienna and Prague. The British and French had also decided that Hitler had politically beaten them for the last time and so gave assurances of assistance to Poland. The capitals of Europe were witness to much diplomatic activity during the ensuing months. Hitler and Mussolini signed the 'Pact of Steel', confirming their mutual aid if either were attacked. The temperature began to rise once more.

Chamberlain suggested a conference between Poland and the major European powers, however Warsaw would not correspond with Moscow. In the event of war, the Soviet Union had insisted on the right of passage for their troops across Polish territory, Poland refused and before London could convince Poland of the error of their ways, Hitler dealt a political ace card, one that no one had expected.

In May 1939, Stalin replaced his Jewish Foreign Minister, Maxim Litvinov, with Vyacheslav Molotov. Did he believe this move would be favourably received in Berlin? Molotov was certainly more acceptable to the anti-Semitic German Government, in comparison Litvinov had often been referred to in National Socialist circles as 'the Jew Finkelstein'. Before any move on Poland was possible, Hitler needed to know the position of the Soviet Union. Hitler telegraphed Stalin requesting that his Foreign Minister be allowed to visit Moscow to discuss mutual interests. Stalin agreed and the non-aggression pact between the most unlikely partners was signed on 23rd August 1939. A secret appendix to the agreement allowed for a systematic carving up of Polish territory between the two major players, Germany and Russia.

The way was now clear for Hitler to carry out 'Case White', the invasion of Poland and the return of Danzig to Germany. Amidst this flurry of diplomatic and military activity, Heydrich had much to contemplate. Little was he to know that he had just three more years to live.

SOURCES BY CHAPTER

Foreword

1. Berlin Document Centre, Heydrich SSO file
2. Correspondence to authors.
3. Correspondence to authors.

Introduction.

1. Macdonald, *The Killing of SS Obergruppenführer Reinhard Heydrich,* p3.

Chapter One.

1. Stadtarchiv Halle and Deschner, *Heydrich - The Pursuit of Total Power,* p16.
2. Standesamt Halle.
3. Deschner, p19.
4. BDC, *Heydrich SSO file.*
5. BDC, *Heydrich SSO file* and Calic, *Reinhard Heydrich,* p29.

Chapter Two.

1. BDC, *Heydrich SSO file* and Deschner, 23.
2. Correspondence to authors.
3. Deschner, p26.
4. Naval record taken from Deschner and Wighton, *Heydrich, Hitler's Most Evil Henchman.*
5. Höhne, *Canaris,* p38.
6. Lina Heydrich, *Leben mit einem Kriegsverbrecher.*
7. *ibid.*
8. Wighton, p33.
9. Deschner, p30.
10. *ibid,* p30.
11. *ibid,* p31.
12. Lina Heydrich and Deschner, p33.
13. Deschner, p33.
14. Lina Heydrich.
15. Deschner, p34.
16. Lina Heydrich.
17. Original document in private collection.
18. Lina Heydrich and Deschner, p36.

Chapter Three.

1. BDC, *Heydrich SSO file* and SS Dienstaltersliste 1941.
2. BDC, *Heydrich SSO file.*
3. Deschner, p40.
4. *ibid,* p42.
5. BDC, *Heydrich SSO file* and SS Dienstaltersliste 1934.
6. BDC, *Heydrich SSO file.*
7. Lina Heydrich.
8. Deschner, p43.
9. Lina Heydrich.

Chapter Four.

1. Lina Heydrich, letter sent by RH, & Deschner, p49.
2. Lina Heydrich.
3. BDC, *Heydrich SSO file.*
4. Deschner, p49.
5. BDC, *Heydrich SSO file.*
6. Lina Heydrich.
7. Deschner, p55.
8. SS Dienstaltersliste 1944.
9. *ibid*
10. BDC, *Heydrich SSO file* and Deschner, p54.

11. BDC, *Heydrich SSO file.*
12. Deschner, p54.

Chapter Five.
1. BDC, *Heydrich SSO file.*
2. *ibid*
3. Deschner, p62.
4. Hagen, *Die Geheime Front* and Deschner, p62.
5. Kempner, *Eichmann und Komplizen.*
6. Deschner, p62-63.
7. Standesamt Halle.
8. Correspondence to authors.
9. Deschner, p63-65 & Kersten, *The Kersten Memoirs 1940-1945.*
10. *ibid*
11. Trevor-Roper, *Introduction to The Kersten Memoirs* and *The Times* 3/6/62.
12. Höhne, *The Order of the Death's Head,* p142-143.
13. Wighton, p24.
14. BDC, *Heydrich SSO file.*

Chapter Six.
1. Shirer, *The Rise and Fall of the Third Reich,* p166.
2. *ibid,* p172.
3. *ibid,* p187.
4. Lorant, *Sieg Heil!* p212.
5. Höhne, *The Order of the Death's Head,* p76.
6. BDC, *Heydrich SSO file.*
7. Deschner, p74.
8. Höhne, p173.
9. Lina Heydrich.
10. Original document in private archive.
11. Deschner, p71 and Wighton, p49-50.
12. BDC, *Heydrich SSO file,* Aronson, *Reinhard Heydrich und die Frühgeschichte von Gestapo und SD,* Deschner, p70 and Höhne, p77 .
13. Deschner, p74-75.
14. *ibid,* p75.
15. SS Dienstaltersliste 1944.
16. *ibid*
17. Deschner, p76 and Lina Heydrich.
18. Aronson, *Reinhard Heydrich und die Frühgeschichte von Gestapo und SD.*
19. Berben, *Dachau,* p45.
20. Segev, *Soldiers of Evil,* p43, Sydnor, *Soldiers of Destruction,* p10-15 and Berben, p45.
21. Deschner, p78.
22. Lina Heydrich and Deschner, p81.
23. Hagen, *Die Geheime Front,* p86.
24. Deschner, p82.
25. Deschner, p83 and Höhne, p90.
26. BDC, *Heydrich SSO file,* Höhne, p91 and Deschner, p84.
27. Deschner, p85.
28. BDC, *Heydrich SSO file.*
29. *ibid.*
30. *ibid.*
31. Rürup, p65.
32. BDC, *Heydrich SSO file.*
33. Rürup, p21.

Chapter Seven.
1. BDC, *Heydrich SSO file.*
2. Staatsarchiv München, *Nachlass Eberstein.*
3. Göring's testimony before the International Military Tribunal Nuremberg.

4. Deschner, p107 & Höhne, p120.
5. Höhne, p126-127 and Gallo, *The Night of Long Knives,* p270.
6. Tolstoy, *Night of the Long Knives,* p143.
7. Shirer, p223.
8. *ibid,* p226.
9. Original document in private archive.
10. Lina Heydrich.
11. BDC, *Heydrich SSO file.*
12. *ibid.*
13. Deschner, p102.
14. Staatsbibliothek München, *Das Schwarze Korps.*
15. *ibid*
16. Rürup, p58.
17. Höhne, p194.
18. Rürup, p61.
19. *ibid*
20. BDC, *Eicke SSO file.*

Chapter Eight.
1. Peis, *The Man Who Started the War,* p49 & Höhne, p257.
2. Deschner, p129.
3. Höhne, *Canaris,* p166.
4. Lina Heydrich.
4a. The house still stands in a tree-lined road. Neighbours stated that opposite stood temporary wooden buildings which housed the guard. During the night, police patrolled the street. A security map of Heydrich's route to his house can be found in his personal file at the BDC.
5. Höhne, *The Order of the Death's Head,* p261.
6. Irving, *Nuremberg - The Last Battle,* p82.
Note on The Hossbach Memorandum. Hossbach was one of Hitler's adjutants who wrote a memorandum on this meeting 5 days later. Produced in evidence at the trial of the major war criminals at Nuremberg, it was vehemently disputed by Göring.
7. Höhne, p241.
8. *ibid,* p242.
9. Fest, *Hitler,* p542.
10. Höhne, p248.
11. Höhne, p250.
12. MacLean, *Quiet Flows the Rhine,* p101.

Chapter Nine.
1. BDC, *Heydrich SSO file.*
2. Lina Heydrich.
3. *ibid*
4. *ibid*
5. BDC, *Heydrich SSO file.*
6. Lina Heydrich.
7. BDC, *Heydrich SSO file.*
8. Lina Heydrich.
9. *ibid*
10. *ibid*
11. *ibid*
12. SS Dienstaltersliste 1944.
13. Stadtarchiv Halle.
14. Lina Heydrich.
15. *ibid*

Chapter Ten.
1. Photocopy of SS Leitheft article in authors' possession.
2. Deschner, p119.

3. *ibid,* p119-120.
4. *ibid,* p120.
5. *ibid,* p122.
6. *ibid,* p117.
7. *ibid,* p118.
8. *ibid,* p118-119.

Chapter Eleven.
1. Deutsche Allgemeine Zeitung, 1940.
2. Höhne, p226.
3. Höhne, p229.
4. Abshagen, p169.
5. Bundesarchiv Koblenz.
6. Höhne, p234.
7. *ibid,* p235.
8. *ibid,* p236.
9. *ibid,* p304.
10. *ibid,* p255.
11. Bundesarchiv Koblenz.

Chapter Twelve.
1. Shirer, p532.
2. Höhne, p267-274.
3. Shirer, p286.
4. Höhne, p280.
5. Original document in private archive.
6. Shirer, p361.
7. Fest, p553.
8. Shirer, p397.
9. After the Battle No. 62.
10. *ibid*

SS RANKS WITH CLOSEST ENGLISH MILITARY EQUIVALENT

Reichsführer-SS	Head of the entireSS organisation
SS-Oberstgruppenführer	Field Marshal
SS-Obergruppenführer	General
SS-Gruppenführer	Lieutenant-General
SS-Brigadeführer	Major-General
SS-Oberführer	Brigadier
SS-Standartenführer	Brigadier
SS-Obersturmbannführer	Lieutenant-Colonel
SS-Sturmbannführer	Major
SS-Hauptsturmführer	Captain
SS-Obersturmführer	Lieutenant
SS-Untersturmführer	2nd Lieutenant
SS-Stabscharführer	Regimental Sergeant Major
SS-Sturmscharführer	Company Sergeant Major
SS-Hauptscharführer	Staff Sergeant
SS-Oberscharführer	Sergeant
SS-Scharführer	Lance Sergeant
SS-Unterscharführer	Corporal
SS-Rottenführer	Lance Corporal
SS-Sturmmann	Private
SS-Mann	Private

BIBLIOGRAPHY AND SOURCE NOTES

Abshagen, Karl Heinz, *Canaris.* Hutchinson 1956.
Aharoni, Zvi and Dietl, Wilhelm. *Operation Eichmann.* Arms & Armour Press 1996.
Angolia, John R. *Cloth Insignia of the SS.* Bender 1983.
Arad, Yitzhad. *Belzec, Sobibor, Treblinka. The Operation Reinhard Death Camps.* Indiana University Press 1987.
Aronson, Shlomo. *Reinhard Heydrich und die Frühgeschichte von Gestapo und SD.* Stuttgart 1971.
Baynes, Norman. *The Speeches of Adolf Hitler, April 1922-August 1939.* London 1942.
Berben, Paul. *Dachau.* Norfolk Press 1975.
Best, S. Payne. *The Venlo Incident.* 1950.
Black, Peter R. *Ernst Kaltenbrunner.* Princeton University Press 1984.
Bloch, Michael. *Ribbentrop.* Bantam 1992.
Buck, Gerhard. *Das Führerhauptquartier 1939-1945.* Druffel 1983.
Breitman, Richard. *The Architect of Genocide.* The Bodley Head 1991.
Brissaud, Andre. *The Nazi Secret Service.* The Bodley Head 1974.
Browder, George C. *Hitler's Enforcers,* Oxford University Press 1996.
Bullock, Alan. *Hitler: A Study in Tyrrany.* Pelican 1962.
Butler, Rupert. *An Illustrated History of the Gestapo.* Allan 1992.
Calic, Edouard. *Reinhard Heydrich.* Military Heritage Press 1985.
Conot, Robert E. *Justice at Nuremberg.* Carroll and Graf 1984.
Cookridge, E.H. *Gehlen - Spy of the Century.* Corgi 1972.
Crankshaw, Edward. *Gestapo.* Greenhill 1990.
Cross, Colin. *Adolf Hitler.* Coronet 1974.
Cvancara, Jaroslav. *Akce Atentat.* Magnet Press 1993.
Delarue, Jacques. *The History of the Gestapo.* Macdonald 1964.
Deschner, Günther. *Heydrich - The Pursuit of Total Power.* Orbis 1981.
Dornberg, John. *The Putsch That Failed.* Weidenfeld & Nicolson 1982.
Fest, Joachim C. *The Face of the Third Reich.* Pelican 1972.
Fest, Joachim C. *Hitler.* Ullstein 1973.
Fleming, Gerald. *Hitler and the Final Solution.* Hamilton 1984.
Frischauer, Willi. *Himmler.* Odhams Press 1953.
Gallo, Max. *The Night of Long Knives.* Souvenir Press 1973.
Gilbert, Martin. *The Holocaust.* Collins 1986.
Goldhagen, Daniel J. *Hitler's Willing Executioners.* Little Brown 1996.
Graber, G.S. *The Life and Times of Reinhard Heydrich.* Hale 1981.
Hagen, Walter (Höttl, Wilhelm). *Die Geheime Front.* 1950.
Hamilton, Charles. *Leaders & Personalities of the Third Reich.* Bender 1984.
Hamilton, Charles. *Leaders & Personalities of the Third Reich (vol. II).* Bender 1996.
Headland, Ronald. *Messages of Murder.* Associated University Presses 1992.
Heiber, Helmut. *Goebbels.* Robert Hale 1973.
Heiber, Helmut. *Reichsführer! Briefe an und von Himmler.* Deutsche 1968.
Heydrich, Lina. *Leben mit einem Kriegsverbrecher.* Ludwig 1976.
Hoffmann, Peter. *Hitler's Personal Security.* Macmillan 1979.
Höhne, Heinz. *The Order of the Death's Head.* Coward-McCann 1970.
Höhne, Heinz. *Canaris.* Secker & Warburg 1979.
Höss, Rudolf. *Commandant of Auschwitz.* Pan 1961.
Irving, David. *Göring.* Avon 1990.
Irving, David. *Hitler's War.* Focal Point 1991.
Irving, David. *Nuremberg - The Last Battle.* Focal Point 1996.
Irving, David. *Goebbels - Mastermind of the Third Reich.* Focal Point 1996.
Ivanov, Miroslav. *The Assassination of Heydrich.* Hart-Davis MacGibbon 1973.
Ivanov, Miroslav. *Der Henker von Prag.* Edition Q 1993.
Kemp, Anthony. *The Secret Hunters.* O'Mara 1986.
Kempner, Robert. *Eichmann und Komplizen.* 1961.
Kersten, Felix. *The Kersten Memoirs 1940-1945.* Hutchinson 1956.
Kessler, Leo. *Betrayal at Venlo.* Cooper 1991.
Koch, Peter-Ferdinand. *Himmlers Graue Eminenz - Oswald Pohl.* Facta Oblita 1988.

Krausnick, Helmut and Broszat, Martin. *Anatomy of the SS State.* Paladin 1970.
Krausnik, Helmut. *Hitlers Einsatzgruppen.* Fischer 1985.
Lang, Jochen von. *Bormann.* Book Club Associates 1979.
Lang, Jochen von. *Eichmann Interrogated.* The Bodley Head 1983.
Le Chene, Evelyn. *Mauthausen - The History of a Death Camp.* Methuen 1971.
Lochner, Louis. *Goebbels Tagebücher aus den Jahren 1942-1943.* Zurich 1948.
Lorant, Stefan. *Sieg Heil!* Norton & Co. 1974.
MacDonald, Callum. *The Killing of SS-Obergruppenführer Reinhard Heydrich 27 May 1942.* Macmillan 1989.
MacDonald, Callum & Kaplan, Jan. *Prague in the Shadow of the Swastika.* Quartet Books 1995.
MacLean, French L. *Quiet Flows the Rhine,* Fedorowicz 1996.
Marrus, Michael R. *The Nuremberg War Crimes Trial 1945-46,* Bedford 1997.
Moczarski, Kazimirerz. *Conversations with an Executioner.* Prentice Hall 1981.
Mollo, Andrew. *A Pictorial History of the SS 1923-1945.* Macdonald & Jane's 1976.
Mollo, Andrew. *Uniforms of the SS. Volume 5.* Historical Research Unit 1992.
Overy, R.J. *Goering The Iron Man.* Routledge & Kegan Paul 1984.
Padfield, Peter. *Himmler - Reichsführer SS.* Papermac 1991.
Pätzold, Kurt and Schwarz, Erika. *Tagesordnung: Judenmord.* Metropol 1992.
Peis, Gunter. *The Man Who Started The War.* Odhams 1960.
Preradovich, Nikolaus von. *Die Generale der Waffen SS.* Vowinckel 1985.
Reitlinger, Gerald. *The Final Solution.* Beechhurst 1953.
Reitlinger, Gerald. *The SS - Alibi of a Nation 1922-1945.* Arms & Armour Press 1981.
Rürup, Reinhard. *Der Krieg gegen die Sowjetunion 1941-1945.* Argon 1991.
Rürup, Reinhard. *Topography of Terror.* Arenhövel 1989.
Russell, Stuart & Schneider, Jost W. *Heinrich Himmlers Burg.* Heitz & Höffkes 1989.
Segev, Tom. *Soldiers of Evil.* Grafton 1990.
Safrian, Hans. *Eichmann und seine Gehilfen.* Fischer 1995.
Schellenberg, Walter. *The Schellenberg Memoirs.* Andre Deutsch 1956.
Schneider, Jost W. *Verleihung Genehmigt! Their Honour was Loyalty!* Bender 1993.
Shirer, William L. *The Rise and Fall of the Third Reich.* Book Club Associates 1985.
Smelser, R. and Zitelmann, R. *Die Braune Elite (vol. I),* Wissenschaftliche Buchgesellschaft 1989.
Smelser, R., Syring, E. and Zitelmann, R. *Die Braune Elite (vol. II),* Wissenschaftliche Buchgesellschaft 1993.
Sydnor Jr., Charles W. *Soldiers of Destruction.* Guild 1989.
Thalmann, Rita & Feinermann, Emmanuel. *Crystal Night.* Thames & Hudson 1974.
Toland, John. *Adolf Hitler.* Doubleday 1976.
Tolstoy, Nikolai. *Night of the Long Knives.* Ballantine's 1972.
Trevor-Roper, H.R. *The Bormann Letters.* Weidenfeld & Nicolson 1954.
Trevor-Roper, H.R. *The Last Days of Hitler.* Collier 1966.
Tuchel, Johannes. *Am Grossen Wannsee 56-58.* Edition Hentrich 1992.
Ulric of England. *Deutschland Erwache.* Bender 1997.
Wiener, Jan. *The Assassination of Heydrich.* Grossman 1969.
Wighton, Charles. *Heydrich - Hitler's Most Evil Henchman.* Chilton 1962.
Wykes, Alan. *Himmler.* Ballantine's 1972.
Yerger, Marc C. *Allgemeine SS.* Schiffer 1997.

OTHER SOURCES

Dienstaltersliste der Schutzstaffel der NSDAP. October 1934.
Dienstaltersliste der Schutzstaffel der NSDAP. July 1935.
Dienstaltersliste der Schutzstaffel der NSDAP. December 1938.
Dienstaltersliste der Schutzstaffel der NSDAP. 1941.
Dienstaltersliste der Schutzstaffel der NSDAP. October / November 1944.
Dienstaltersliste der Waffen-SS. July 1944. New edition Biblio Verlag 1987.
Reinhard Heydrich. Reichssicherheitshauptamt IB1. Ahnenerbe Stiftung Verlag 1943.
Reinhard Heydrich. (English Translation) Ulric of England Research Unit 1993.
After The Battle. Numbers 24, 56, 61 and 62. Battle of Britain Prints International.
Das Spiel ist aus - Arthur Nebe. Der Spiegel 1950.

Das Attentat auf Reinhard Heydrich vom 27 Mai 1942. Ein Bericht des Kriminalrats Heinz Pannwitz. Stanislav F. Berton in Vierteljahrshefte für Zeitgeschichte 1985.
The Assassination of Reinhard Heydrich. Richard A. Davis, MD, FACS. 1971.
Das Schwarze Korps. 1935-1942.
Deutsche Allgemeine Zeitung, 1940.
Allgemeines Liederbuch der SS.
Fehmarnsches Tageblatt. 1969.
Die Deutsche Polizei. 1942.
Deutsche Zeitung im Ostland, 1942.
The London Times. 1962.

ARCHIVES CONSULTED FOR DOCUMENTS & PERIODICALS

Bundesarchiv Koblenz.
Berlin Document Centre.
Stadtarchiv Berlin.
Stadtarchiv Halle.
Standesamt Halle.
Stadtarchiv Kiel.
Stadtarchiv Burg a. Fehmarn.
Bayerisches Staatsarchiv Munich.
Institut für Zeitgeschichte Munich.
Staatsbibliothek Munich.
Czech Army Archives Prague.
State Archives Prague.
Imperial War Museum London.
Public Records Office London.
Yivo Institute New York.
National Archives Washington DC.
Various archives in private hands.

With the onset of the Second World War, Heydrich braved the air with Luftwaffe fighter group JG 1, however his flying days were short lived. After crash landing behind Soviet lines, but managing to return to Germany unharmed , Hitler forbid Heydrich from flying with the Luftwaffe again. Desk bound for the duration of the war, Heydrich had much work to address, particularly since the issue of the 'Jewish Question' largely came under his jurisdiction.

Hitler meanwhile had been unhappy with the running of the protectorate of Bohemia & Moravia, instructing the existing 'Reichsprotecktor', Von Neurath, to return to Germany. Remarkably, Hitler gave Heydrich this important position. Heydrich arrived in Prague on 27th September 1941.

What were the circumstances which resulted in Great Britain, less than one year later, having Deputy-Reichsprotector Heydrich assassinated? Furthermore, what became of his wife and family immediately after his death and in the aftermath of the Second World War ?

ISBN 0 9537577 6 5

Volume II will be available from the Autumn of 2002.

OTHER TITLES FROM ULRIC PUBLISHING

GERMAN MILITARY TIMEPIECES OF W.W.II VOLUME 1
ISBN 0 9529103 0 6
£12.99

GERMAN MILITARY TIMEPIECES OF W.W.II VOLUME 2
ISBN 0 9529103 6 5
£24.99

A COLLECTORS GUIDE TO SS & POLITICAL CUFFBANDS
ISBN 0 9529103 5 7
£18.00
(OUT OF PRINT)

COLLECTING THIRD REICH RECORDINGS
ISBN 0 9537577 2 2
£19.95

THE SS FAMILY
(PROCEDURES FOR CONDUCTING FAMILY CELEBRATIONS)
ISBN 0 9529103 1 4
£18.00

REINHARD HEYDRICH MEMORIAL BOOK
ISBN 0 9529103 2 2
£14.99

LEADERS OF THE THIRD REICH
ISBN 9529103 7 3
£9.95

1934 DIENSTALTERSLISTE – THE 1934 SS OFFICER RANK LIST
ISBN 0 9529103 3 0
£24.99

1944 DIENSTALTERSLISTE – THE 1944 SS OFFICER RANK LIST
ISBN 0 9529103 8 1
£49.99

THIRD REICH PRICE GUIDE
(TWICE YEARLY)
ISBN VARIOUS
£9.50

ORDER THROUGH ANY GOOD BOOKSHOP OR DIRECT FROM ULRIC PUBLISHING

PO BOX 55 CHURCH STRETTON SHROPSHIRE SY6 6WR ENGLAND
www.ulric-publishing.com
e-mail
books@ulric-publishing.com

USA DISTRIBUTION
R.JAMES BENDER PUBLISHING PO BOX 23456 SAN JOSE CA 153-3456 USA